THE
DEATH
MYTH

THE DEATH MYTH

Uncovering What the Bible Really
Says about the Afterlife

BRIAN M. ROSSITER

THE DEATH MYTH
UNCOVERING WHAT THE BIBLE REALLY SAYS ABOUT THE AFTERLIFE

Unless otherwise noted, all quotations of the Old and New Testament are from the HOLY BIBLE, NEW INTERNATIONAL VERSION®. NIV® Copyright © 1973, 1978, 1984 by International Bible Society. Used by permission of Zondervan. All rights reserved.

iUniverse books may be ordered through booksellers or by contacting:

iUniverse
1663 Liberty Drive
Bloomington, IN 47403
www.iuniverse.com
1-800-Authors (1-800-288-4677)

Because of the dynamic nature of the Internet, any web addresses or links contained in this book may have changed since publication and may no longer be valid. The views expressed in this work are solely those of the author and do not necessarily reflect the views of the publisher, and the publisher hereby disclaims any responsibility for them.

Any people depicted in stock imagery provided by Thinkstock are models, and such images are being used for illustrative purposes only. Certain stock imagery © Thinkstock.

ISBN: 978-1-5320-3470-1 (sc)
ISBN: 978-1-5320-3469-5 (e)

Library of Congress Control Number: 2017918045

Print information available on the last page.

iUniverse rev. date: 12/19/2017

CONTENTS

ACKNOWLEDGEMENTS

I would first like to thank the Lord Jesus Christ for providing me with both the inspiration and the motivation to write this book. I would like to thank my wife, Jessi, for her patience and support in the process of bringing this project to completion. Lastly, I would like to thank my brother and best friend, Wayne Rossiter, for the countless discussions and ideas that ultimately helped to shape this book's contents.

PREFACE

As you pass through the wooden doors and begin to make your way across the dimly-lit hallway, you say a solemn hello to friends and relatives you haven't seen in years. A handshake here, a "how you been?" there. Meanwhile, a somber mix of piano and violin plays in the background through the house speakers. After the brief family reunion, you manage to find your way to a vacant seat. Minutes creep by as if they are aware of their own passing. By the time that casual pleasantry begins to bleed into awkward silence, the reverend takes his podium. As he starts to speak his first few carefully chosen words, you become completely in tune with the gravity of the situation. *This is a funeral*; a real person, like you or me, has left this world forever.

A prayer invites God to enter the building, and even the skeptics hope (if only for a second) to feel something "spiritual." You begin to hear about the person lying in the casket—where she lived, how long she experienced life, and who she is leaving behind. You quickly glance up to the front row in order to evaluate the condition of the immediate family. The momentary trance ends as the familiar words of Psalm 23 bring you back to focus: "The Lord is my shepherd; I shall not want. He makes me lie down in green pastures. He leads me beside still waters." A relative comes up to read his favorite passage of Scripture and provide some personal details about the deceased person that most people in the room were not previously privy to. More passages are read, and you are asked to evaluate your own perspective on eternity. Finally, you hear some long overdue words of encouragement. "We know that she is in a better place: somewhere far away from the trials and difficulties of this world. Having gone on to glory, she is now with the Lord."

Most of us have been in this situation before, and heard similar teachings. It's commonplace at Christian funerals around the globe. It's comforting. It's powerful. It's *traditional*. But the critical question remains: is it true? Will we go on to "be with the Lord" immediately when we die? If so, will we live as disembodied souls or embodied beings? How will it happen? What will it be like? What exactly *does* the Bible say about the afterlife?

It has long been known that there are really only two types of people—those who have died, and those who will. I feel as though I faced my own mortality at a very young age. I was afraid of death before I even understood all that it entails. The death of a schoolmate disturbed me in the 5th grade, as did the passing of my paternal grandparents in subsequent years. I can recall a number of sleepless nights from my high school days, many of them due to my own concerns about the fleeting nature of life. Throughout my twenties, I became almost emotionally paralyzed by the problem on more than one occasion. Typically, this was either due to the passing of those around me or my own personal health concerns. The birth of my daughter brought about an even greater sense of self-preservation; all else aside, I wanted to be around for her and my wife, and I sometimes feared that I wouldn't be. Though I feel a much greater sense of peace today than I once did, these difficulties still rear their ugly heads on occasion.

In case you haven't picked up on it, I am afraid of death. The reason why is simple: death is the absence of life, and all we have ever known is life. No one among us knows to an absolute certainty what will happen when we depart from this world. Even those who claim to know simply don't. Not for sure. This is why the apostle Paul often referred to Christ's return and the resurrection as a matter of *hope*. While we have good reason to believe in the resurrection and the prospect of everlasting life, we will only know for sure on the day when we receive these gifts. The apostle Paul made the case that if Christ was not raised from the dead, then we should be pitied above all people (1 Cor. 15:19). I think he ultimately meant this in a very personal way—if Christ did not conquer the grave then neither will we. If we will not conquer death, then we have lived our lives in service to something that doesn't even exist. I agree: if that were the case, we should be pitied.

It is this prospect that caused the author of Ecclesiastes (Qohelet)[1] to mourn his own existence, feeling that the day of death is better than the day of birth (7:1). I suppose the reason he felt this way is that the dead don't have

---

[1] The author of Ecclesiastes identifies himself as "Qohelet," which is a title, not a given name. The name literally translates to the "assembler," but is commonly translated in English as the "preacher" or the "teacher." Whatever the case, he is one who is thought to instruct the assembly of believers. See Crenshaw's, *An Introduction to the Old Testament*, 247-250 for further discussion about the author of Ecclesiastes.

to consider their own mortality. Try as he might to find it, he understood that the hope for any lasting meaning in life evaporates without the prospect of the afterlife. Qohelet got it—he understood. If death is the end of the human story, then nothing in life ultimately makes any difference at all. We all become crash test dummies; as we charge towards the brick wall ahead, we concern ourselves with the smell of the air freshener beneath the rearview mirror. All the while, we know it makes no difference whatsoever. Vanity of vanities . . . all is vanity.[2]

All of this is intended to drive home one unmistakable point—death is a serious matter. I would argue that an honest fear of death is actually quite healthy. Perhaps those who never struggle with the problem are the ones that need to be evaluated. As I have so often told students, it is only when we recognize the problem that we can fully appreciate the solution. While I typically mean this with regards to the effects of the Fall of man and the good news of Jesus Christ, the issue of death is no different.

Though the topic of death captivates many of us, I am not attempting to prove that we possess a "soul," a "mind," or anything beyond the materialist's perspective on life. Instead, I am assuming that we all possess something of the sort. In this, I understand that I am assuming much. Discussions about the nature of the human soul and whether or not such a thing actually exists have long been subjects of debate in both secular and religious circles. For the most part, the Judeo-Christian tradition has always affirmed the existence of a component or quality of human existence that is distinct from the physical body. Typically, religious believers of nearly all stripes refer to this quality or component as the "soul." Now, as I will actually seek to demonstrate, the majority view is certainly not always the correct one. Simply saying that something is correct because it is the "traditional" view or the "majority" view can be extremely problematic. Tradition is a fine thing . . . in moderation. I will differ with many interpretations and ideologies concerning the soul, specifically any notion that the soul is consciously separable from the body, superior to the body, or that it can somehow exist on its own. In contrast, my view is that the soul is an appropriate term for the information and the memories that characterize each of us.[3]

---

[2] The word we translate as "vanity" is the Hebrew term *hă·ḇel*. This term is better translated as "vapor" or "breath," as it refers here to the passing nature of this life and all that it entails. This is the problem that the book of Ecclesiastes really deals with—the reality that life is fleeting, and death waits just around the bend.

[3] I explain this concept in great detail in chapter four, the "Death Blow."

Therefore, I find it to be neither logical nor scriptural to completely jettison all notions of the soul, *so long as we are very clear about its nature*. Further, I believe that at least a minimal commitment to the idea of the soul is necessary in any proper and comprehensive understanding of both human existence and the afterlife. I trust that my reasons for feeling this way will become apparent throughout the book. With this in mind, I will not dedicate extensive time—and it would take extensive time—attempting to prove to the secular world that the soul exists in any way, shape, or form. Throughout this book, I will reference a number of authors who have sought to do that very thing. This being said, I am predominantly writing this book to my fellow Christians. However, parts of it will no doubt be interesting to anyone who is intrigued by the topics of death and the afterlife. This is especially true because I will be evaluating what the most famous religious text in history says about all of this. I of course mean the Bible.

My specific goals with this book are very modest, for the most part anyway. My first goal is to provide a solid sketch of the key terms and issues involved in the discussion of the afterlife, without getting completely bogged down in the marsh of theological jargon. As complex as the subject is, many have become so obsessed with analyzing every perspective on the horizon that they miss the "forest" for the "trees." I want this book to be detailed enough to grasp the issue and to do it justice, without making it completely overwhelming. My second goal is to show that the issue of what happens at death is most definitely still up for debate. In this, the "traditional view" of the afterlife is called into question in a variety of ways. Finally—and this is my least modest goal of the three—I hope to demonstrate that my view of the subject, which I share with many others of both the past and the present, makes the best sense of all the factors as a whole. No view will ever be completely airtight, and I think you will see why when we get into the meat of the biblical text. This does not, however, mean that some views are not more plausible than others. While those are my three specific goals, the most important point of the book is to stir the imagination a bit by asking that you (the reader) assess the matter in as open and honest a way as possible. As I alluded to at the end of the funeral introduction: are the common Christian beliefs about the afterlife actually true?

I believe there is power in knowing the truth, even if we cannot always pinpoint why it is so. More importantly, the most widely held beliefs about the issue can (and do, I think) lead people to some dangerous views about our world and our faith. With that said, I most specifically wrote this book for all who share my desire to search for what is genuine, and it is also why I have called it *The Death Myth*. In researching all of the issues you are about to read, I came to the conclusion that the truth of the matter is that parts of the church—consisting of its immense body of believers and its rich heritage—have propagated a myth about the afterlife, and many have unknowingly accepted it.

Chances are that *you* (whoever *you* are) have also been lied to. This is probably not a lie coming from malice (though it occasionally may be), but typically one emerging from a willingness to just accept whatever we are told, without personal investigation or free thought. You see, I think it is quite likely that none of us will die and go to heaven. At least, not in the way we are usually told it will happen. All who call upon the name of Christ will indeed live with him for the rest of eternity after death. But again, *not in the way most of us have been taught*. Bold words, I know. So, I now end the introduction to this book with a statement of sincerity. Whether you end up agreeing with me or not, I hope that this book can serve to lead you towards the truth about the afterlife and to the God who will bring us into His eternal Kingdom.

CHAPTER ONE

LAYING THE FOUNDATION

I n order to lay the foundation for the rest of the book, it will be essential to do a bit of investigative legwork. First and foremost, it is necessary to provide some historical context of the situation and to define the essential terms of the discussion. The second priority is to evaluate the realities of the body and the soul, since these two concepts are absolutely crucial in understanding the logistics of the afterlife. While parts of the introduction (and sections of the entire book, for that matter) may appear to be somewhat technical, I assure you that they are necessary. I have made a conscious effort to cover only the most essential aspects of the issue. But make no mistake about it: of all the theological issues one could choose to investigate, our existence in the afterlife ranks near the top of the list in terms of its complexity. Believing I had a good grip on this before I ever thought to write a book, the depth of the situation was even overwhelming for me at points. Hopefully, the following section will be both eye-opening and illustrative of the depth of the topic.

A BRIEF HISTORY OF THOUGHT

One of the truly essentially points that we need to recognize about the different Christian views of the afterlife is that the ultimate hope of a physical, bodily resurrection is the common point of agreement. This is not common in the sense that the majority of modern Christians acknowledge this point (they no longer do), but common in the sense that every respectable Christian scholar should recognize that this is so. If you doubt this reality—that we will be raised from the dead and given new bodies—then hopefully it will become apparent throughout the course of this book. With the belief in a bodily resurrection taken as an *a priori*—but biblically undeniable—assumption, I am chiefly concerned with discussing what happens in the meantime: the time between our deaths and our resurrections.

If there is a space between death and resurrection, how should we understand it? This period is frequently referred to as the "intermediate state of the dead," or simply the "interim period."[4] A solid read of the contemporary literature that discusses the afterlife yields quite a number of different views about what happens immediately after death,[5] but it can be very easy to overcomplicate the options. On the other hand, this issue can also be oversimplified. Typically, this can occur whenever one attempts to act as though heaven and hell are the only possible destinations for the "conscious dead" (note the oxymoron) that the Bible portrays throughout its pages. I will discuss this problem in more detail later on.

For all intents and purposes, there are essentially three general ways that a Christian could view the state of the dead. In that simple statement, I realize that I have already created a problem for many readers. Most Christians (particularly of the western church variety) have been assured—*absolutely assured*—that our souls will soar off to heaven when our "lowly bodies" finally give out. This view, which is the first option of the afterlife, is that death brings about the soul's departure to either heaven or hell. We die, but our souls continue to consciously live. A scarce minority of people hold that this will occur with a resurrection body (the "immediate resurrection position"), but most see this as a disembodied, immaterial existence. While that option is probably obvious to most of us, the second possibility may not be. The reality is that the Bible also portrays another way of thinking about a disembodied existence after death. In general, the second option can be viewed as another intermediate reality between this life and the one that each of us will ultimately experience after the great judgment. This is not heaven

---

[4] For further clarification, the "intermediate state" refers to the time between this life and the next: between this body, and the one that will later mark our existence at the resurrection. The very question of this book has to do with whether or not this period is marked by a conscious or unconsciousness existence.

[5] Haberas and Moreland, for example, provide an account of six different perspectives on the matter. Some of these views, however, are not overly distinct from one another. In the end, they simply make a classification of two primary categories of thought: those promoting a "conscious state" and those promoting an "unconscious state." *Beyond Death*, 222-230

or hell, but a different existence altogether. All of chapter three is dedicated to evaluating this option, so I will spend no more time describing it here.

In both of the aforementioned views of the afterlife, the human soul is thought to consciously survive death in a disembodied state of existence. Theologians J.P. Moreland and Scott Rae have referred to this view as the *temporary-disembodiment position.*[6] This will be a crucial term to remember as you continue reading. I believe that this is a fitting name for this particular view, and I will use this terminology throughout the course of the book to describe any view in which the soul is believed to consciously exist independent of the body during the interim period.

I also agree with Moreland and Rae that the temporary-disembodiment position (the TDP, from here on) has been the most commonly (i.e. traditionally) held position within the church for nearly two millennia. On the whole, more Christians have believed that the soul consciously survives the death of the body than have not. But I would add that contemporary proponents of this position often depict it in a significantly different way than most Christians would. But I will return to that point later on. For now, it is important to understand that most Christians—whether of the past or present—would agree with the TDP's basic principle that the human soul continues to live when we die. I will repeatedly reference this position, as it is the view that I challenge throughout the book. It is this view that I have called *The Death Myth*.

Some of the greatest theologians of the early church set out to answer the question of what happens when we die. This was not a debate over whether or not believers would ultimately reign with Christ, which all Christians should agree upon, but was instead about *when* and *how* this would occur. The discussion still centers on these concerns. Frequently, their personal studies about these issues led them to ascribe to the belief in the *immortality of the soul.* The immortality of the soul is exactly what it appears to be—the belief that the human soul is immortal, though the body is not. Within this, the soul is viewed as being something that is perhaps capable of existing prior to our lives on earth (particularly in certain Greek philosophies), and is certainly believed to be able to survive apart from the body after death. The soul's existence apart from the body is always viewed as a conscious one, which is of particular interest when discussing the state of the dead. The early church

---

[6] Refer to J.P. Moreland and Scott Rae's *Body and Soul*, 26-40, for a discussion of this perspective and several others.

father Origen (185–254) discussed this concept at a synod in Arabia, but focused so heavily on the immaterial nature of humanity that he ended up rejecting the idea that we would ever be given resurrection bodies.[7] Most of what we read from the renowned theologian Augustine is consistent with the belief in the immortal soul,[8] which has all but assured many of its legitimacy. I mean, who can question the great Augustine?

As with many early church theologians, Platonic—a term deriving from many of the views promoted by the famous Greek philosopher, Plato—beliefs about the soul weighed heavily in the thoughts of both Origen and Augustine. In his critically acclaimed book, *The Passion of the Western Mind*, Richard Tarnas admirably summarized this fascination with Plato:

> ". . . It was Augustine's formulation of Christian Platonism that was to permeate virtually all of medieval Christian thought in the West. So enthusiastic was the Christian integration of the Greek spirit that Socrates and Plato were frequently regarded as divinely inspired pre-Christian saints . . ."[9]

The Greek philosopher Plato was no doubt brilliant in many respects, but he also had a view of existence that was often radically different than the one promoted within the Bible. Among other things, Plato is known for his belief that the physical world around us is something like an image or a copy of the greater, transcendent realms of existence. It is not a good and wonderful thing, as the Bible suggests, but is more like a barrier of sorts. In his famous work the *Phaedo*, Plato—while often speaking through Socrates—alludes to the body as being a burden to the soul, as it prevents the soul from exploring the highest and unchanging objects of all knowledge, called the "Forms." While his views concerning the nature of the soul are most prominent in the *Phaedo*, his negativity towards the body and the material world are evident within his writings as a whole. Few would disagree that Plato emphasized the immaterial above the material.

It was not only Augustine and Origen who were enamored with Plato's conception of the soul. The early church thinker Tertullian unashamedly

---

[7] "Origen, Unorthodox Church Father."

[8] Naoki Kamimura, "Augustine's Understanding of the Soul, the Immortality, and the Being in De Immortalitate Animae."

[9] Richard Tarnas, *The Passion of the Western Mind*, 103.

showed his agreement with the Platonic conception of the immortal soul, saying, "For some things are known even by nature: the immortality of the soul, for instance, is held by many . . . I may use, therefore, the opinion of a Plato, when he declares, 'Every soul is immortal'."[10] True to the ideologies that gave power to the view, implicit in most (if not all) perspectives about the immorality of the soul is the belief that the soul is superior to the body. Ultimately, the soul ends up becoming its own being rather than part of what makes a living being. The soul end up being "us," while the body ends up being virtually unnecessary.

Though the more Platonic conceptions of the immortal soul certainly view the soul in precisely this way, the church has adopted more of this way of thinking than most of us know. I would suggest that this perspective—the belief that the soul is its own being and is superior to the body—comes part and parcel with the TDP, though its supporters tend to believe that their perspectives are leagues apart from Platonic ideas on the matter. It would seem then that the belief in the immortal soul was, on the whole, the majority view throughout most of the post-apostolic church period. Yet, there was certainly no consensus concerning the details of the afterlife. Near the turn of the first century, Clement of Rome[11] spoke of the interim period as a time of *sleep*, in which the faithful await Christ's return.[12] The Apostolic Father Papias also seemed to indicate that life after death was best associated with the events surrounding the return of Christ rather than a conscious interim period.[13] These early sources show us that the first couple centuries of church history witnessed a number of prominent thinkers who differed in their understanding of the state of the dead. To evaluate how proceeding generations of theologians would view this issue, we will move to discussing the aforementioned "third view" of the afterlife.

The final possibility about the interim period is that our bodies return to the ground and our souls return to God, so that the time between death and the return of Christ is characterized by a state of *unconsciousness*. In other words, this view holds that conscious existence temporarily ceases at death, until the resurrection brings us back to life. Throughout history, this view has been most commonly characterized by a doctrine called *soul*

---

[10] Tertullian, *On the Resurrection of the Flesh*, Chapter 3.

[11] Clement is also referred to as Pope Clement or St. Clement I, based on the early church tradition that he was the first Bishop of Rome.

[12] Clement, *The First Epistle of Clement to the Corinthians*, cc. XXVI and XXXV.

[13] *Fragments of Papias*, cc. 4-5.

sleep. Soul sleep was initially popularized when John Calvin, the founder of Calvinism and modern-day Reformed Theology, wrote against specific views of this doctrine in the mid-1530's (AD). Certainly, the discussion of what happens when we die goes back much further, as evidenced by the writings of Clement, Augustine, and the others mentioned above. As we will see, this subject was already being hotly debated within the works of the New Testament. It was in the 16th century, however, that the discussion reached a climax in post-apostolic Christianity, with the doctrine of soul sleep being at the center.

It was near the time of the Protestant Reformation that John Calvin was waging war against this belief. On one particular occasion, Calvin wrote a letter entitled, *Psychopannychia,* which was tediously subtitled: *A Refutation of the Error Entertained by Some Unskillful Persons, Who Ignorantly Imagine that in the Interval between Death and the Judgment the Soul Sleeps.*[14] It has been suggested that the Reformation was a time when two concepts were discussed in relation to the soul sleep doctrine—psychosomnolence and thnetopsychism.[15] These terms are much easier to understand than they appear. The former describes the notion that the soul "sleeps" until the resurrection, and the latter suggests that the body and soul both die and then rise again.

To Calvin, the belief that the soul ceases to consciously exist at death was truly evil. He even went so far as to compare this line of thinking to "cancer:" the spread of a horrid disease.[16] At this point in history, there were apparently a large enough number of people who believed in the doctrine of soul sleep to warrant a response from Calvin. In particular, Calvin's quarrel was with those who were teaching that the soul dies just as the body does.[17] While Calvin is a well-known Reformer who opposed the doctrine of soul sleep, few are aware that the beliefs behind this view were actually upheld by a number of Protestant greats during this period.

Very near to time of the Reformation, the Roman Catholic Church believed the doctrine of soul sleep to be so much a threat to "orthodoxy"

---

[14] John Calvin, *Tracts & Letters – Psychopannychia.*

[15] Conti, "Religio Medici's Profession of Faith."

[16] John Calvin, *Tracts & Letters – Psychopannychia.*

[17] This is similar to the modern-day "recreation position," in which the resurrection is thought to be a recreation of the person because a human being is mainly viewed as being his/her body. When the body dies, the person completely goes extinct. This view does not permit much (if any) possibility of any sort genuine continuity between this life and the next.

(right or proper teaching) that it was officially condemned as *heresy* by the Fifth Council of the Lateran (1512-1517):

> "Whereas some have dared to assert concerning the nature of the reasonable soul that it is mortal, we, with the approbation of the sacred council do condemn and reprobate all those who assert that the intellectual soul is mortal, seeing, according to the canon of Pope Clement V, that the soul is [. . .] immortal [. . .] and we decree that all who adhere to like erroneous assertions shall be shunned and punished as heretics."[18]

It has been argued that the council's decision was more a refutation of the theory of "double truth" than it was a dogmatic view of the immortal nature of the soul,[19] but there can be little doubt that the council supported the immortality of the soul.[20] In a very real sense, the debate over the state of the dead was an immensely important one between the Reformers and the Roman Catholic Church. Since the time of the Reformers and the Lateran decision, the doctrine of soul sleep has continued to be viewed in a rather negative light. The reasons why the doctrine has been so staunchly opposed are somewhat more of a mystery, but it's worth mentioning that you cannot accept indulgences or pray for the well-being of unconscious souls. In the final section of this book, I discuss what I believe to be the other reasons for this hostility. The overall disdain for the soul sleep position caused its supporters to opt for the name "Christian Mortalism," in the hopes of shedding its historical skepticism.[21]

    While I argue within this book that the doctrine actually has its formation

---

[18] "Fifth Lateran Council," session 8.

[19] The "double truth" theory posits that both philosophical and theological pursuits can potentially lead to different conclusions without creating devastating contradictions on either side. See Constant's article, "A Reinterpretation of the Fifth Lateran Council Decree Apostolicd Regiminis (1513)," for a detailed perspective on the Lateran decision.

[20] Ibid. "Session 8" makes this very clear. Among other proofs, one section reads, "For the soul not only truly exists of itself and essentially as the form of the human body . . . but it is also immortal . . ."

[21] For a more thorough account of this issue, I refer you to Norman Burns', *Christian Mortalism from Tyndale to Milton.*

within the Bible itself, it was also advocated by some of the more significant Reformation leaders during the clash with the Catholic Church and its Papacy. Not surprisingly, the man who is perhaps the most famous opponent of the Roman Catholic Church, Martin Luther, actually supported the doctrine of soul sleep. Whether this was out of spite or a genuine belief in the evidence of the doctrine, we may never fully know, but his reasons appear to be biblical in nature. Concerning death, Luther wrote: "Salomon judgeth that the dead are a sleepe, and feele nothing at all. For the dead lye there accompting neyther dayes nor yeares, but when are awaked, they shall seeme to have slept scarce one minute."[22] As depicted in texts like Psalms 90:4 and 2 Peter 3:8, Luther made further reference to the biblical concept that our view of time during the interim period is nothing like God's:

> "As soon as thy eyes have closed shalt thou be woken, a thousand years shall be as if thou hadst slept but a little half hour. Just as at night we hear the clock strike and know not how long we have slept, so too, and how much more, are in death a thousand years soon past. Before a man should turn round, he is already a fair angel."[23]

This clarifies Luther's belief that everlasting life with Christ will be instantaneously *realized* by those who have died, even if thousands of years were to pass (in the view of the living) in the meantime. While his faithfulness to the soul sleep doctrine has been questioned by some, Luther's overall theological position clearly demonstrated a support for the belief.

There are, of course, other very notable Reformers who agreed. John Wycliffe, who has been called the "Morning Star" of the Reformation, is best known for his insistence on the need for the Bible to be translated into English.[24] William Tyndale is credited for creating the first English translation of the Bible from the original (Greek and Hebrew) languages. Both were (and are) highly respected biblical scholars, and both taught that the dead remain unconscious until the resurrection. On a more somber note, both men also lost their lives in the struggle to provide the world with access to the Bible. These men represent quite a powerful trio of theologians and

---

[22] Martin Luther, "An Exposition of Salomon's Booke, called Ecclesiastes or the Preacher."

[23] Martin Luther, *WA*, 37.191.

[24] R.G. Clouse, *Evangelical Dictionary of Biblical Theology*, 1304-5.

church figures. Martin Luther, John Wycliffe, and William Tyndale all held the belief that human beings remain in an unconscious state of existence during the interim period. Of course, no one likes to talk about it. But we could add thinkers like John Locke, Thomas Hobbes, and Edmund Law to that list. While *many* others could be mentioned,[25] it is already clear that some of the most respected intellectuals and figures of Protestant history accepted and promoted an unconscious state of the dead. It is not simply a belief for the heretical, as some parts of the church may suggest.

To this very day, the doctrine of soul sleep is often mocked by believers from a large number of denominational backgrounds. The majority of Christians hold to some type of belief in the immortality of the soul. Regardless of whether or not they would use such terminology, they at least affirm most of its theological tenets. The question of whether or not a soul can exist prior to our entrance into this world—which is certainly what many ancient philosophies taught—is nonessential in a discussion about the state of the dead. In plainest terms, a soul that can exist as its own being, independent of the body, *is* an "immortal soul." Certainly, most parts of the church base their doctrines of the afterlife on this basic belief.

Though the "traditional" Protestant position entails either a sentence to heaven or hell or a trip to temporary resting places (discussed later), Catholic theology holds that Purgatory is often a necessary purification step prior to our ultimate destination in heaven. In each of these cases, the human soul consciously exists during the interim period. Thus, the immortality of the soul is foundational to the previous perspectives. In order to go on living as a disembodied soul, human beings must possess a soul that is capable of living apart from the body as its own being. We must possess an *immortal soul*. At the present-day, history repeats itself; beliefs concerning the nature of the human soul abound. Even at this point of the book, I hope that the complexity of the matter is already apparent. This is far from being a simple issue that has long been settled within the church, though many religious professionals treat it as such. Again, haven't we all been assured by our teachers, pastors, and Christian friends that the human soul goes to live in heaven after the death of the body?

While there are many more historical avenues we could explore, this

---

[25] I strongly recommend Ball's *The Soul Sleepers* for a more exhaustive account of theologians and thinkers who have affirmed the sleep-death position. Prestidge's, *Asleep in Christ*, is also a good resource in this regard.

provides us with at least a solid sketch of the key terms used in this discussion as well as how it has generally been viewed throughout church history. As important as the church Fathers and Reformers can be in any theological pursuit, we still have the luxury of being able to consult the words of Christ and the biblical authors for ourselves. This is not to say that I will cease to pull others into the conversation from this point forward, or that it is not important to do so. Rather, it is to say that genuine biblical interpretation must be focused on the Bible itself. While countless religious shifts have come and gone, the words of the sacred texts have remained unchanged (at least in any theologically significant way) for the last two thousand years. That being said, the main focus of this book will be to evaluate what the Bible has to say about things. Specifically, I will assess the biblical approach to the state of the dead (i.e. when, where, and how human beings exist after death).

For all intents and purposes, there are three major tasks taken up within the body of this book. The *first* of these tasks is to provide a brief overview of my position on the matter. Yes, prior to taking issue with both the passages of Scripture and the perspectives that have led so many to believe that we will one day live somewhere apart from our bodies, I want to at least offer some compelling reasons why I would dare to challenge these ideas to begin with. In the latter part of the book—after we have gone through the vast majority of the biblical passages concerning the state of the dead—I will describe my own personal view in much more detail. By opening with some of my best evidence, my hope is that you will at least see reason enough to continue reading: why we should be open to challenging the status quo, and perhaps even why "bucking" the mainline traditions may well be in order on this particular issue.

The *second* major task of this book is to put forth my strongest challenges to the *temporary-disembodiment position* (the TDP). Again, this is essentially an umbrella term for any view in which the soul consciously survives on its own during the time between death and the resurrection. This critique will take place throughout chapters two and three, but will be particularly sharp in chapter four, which I have called "the Death Blow." The *final* task will be to discuss the practical implications of our individual views on the state of the dead. You may be shocked to find that the subject has far more to do with our present lives than most of us have ever considered. With this framework in place, the remainder of this chapter will be dedicated to discussing what I feel are the most foundational biblical texts in support of my beliefs about the state of the dead and the afterlife. I will begin with one of the most theologically significant chapters in the entire Bible, and one of my personal favorites.

I'LL FLY AWAY: 1 CORINTHIANS 15

Throughout the course of this book, I will reference certain pieces of biblical information again and again. Specifically, Paul's teachings about the nature of the resurrection in 1 Corinthians 15 will repeatedly come to the forefront of the conversation. This is largely because this chapter provides us with the most comprehensive view of what everlasting existence will be like in all of Scripture; it is Paul's *tour de force* on the physical and spiritual nature of humanity. In light of this point, all other passages that discuss this topic must be viewed (at least in part) with this chapter in mind. Based on its length, detail, and the circumstances surrounding its content, 1 Corinthians 15 offers a wealth of insight into questions that are otherwise indiscernible within shorter and more ambiguous passages. For this reason, I thought it necessary to discuss this chapter in some detail before later referencing its teachings. In this sense, my understanding of this chapter serves as the context for my larger views about the state of the dead.

Nearly everyone—even the teens in your local youth group—has heard the famous church hymn, "I'll Fly Away." Even well into the 21st century, the chorus of this hymn is echoed (in one version or another) every Sunday morning in churches throughout the country; "I'll fly away, oh glory, I'll fly away. When I die, hallelujah by and by, I'll fly away." While it is one of the better-known hymns of the church, it actually contains some rather questionable teachings if you consider its lyrical content. In addition to making the body out to be some type of restrictive tomb for the soul, the song very obviously gives the impression that our souls will consciously depart to heaven when our days on earth are done. As I have already mentioned, this particular belief about the afterlife has probably been adopted by more believers than any of the others. It is almost taken for granted within the church, in general, that life in either heaven or hell is the immediate result of our earthly expiration. I would wager that almost every believer has heard this view espoused somewhere along the lines, whether that be during a Sunday morning sermon, a worship service, a funeral, or elsewhere. While it is commonly advocated, the question remains: is it actually true? Will there be a day when our bodies die and our souls "fly away" to heaven? When we dive into the mind of the apostle Paul, we may be required to question something that is normally considered to be so certain.

In 1 Corinthians 15:45-49, Paul associates the resurrection of the dead with a comparison between Adam and Jesus. This is a common comparison for Paul, as he also uses it to explain the doctrine of justification by faith in Romans 5:12-21. In his reference to Adam, Paul takes us all the way back to the creation account in Genesis 2:7. The key point in this comparison is that Adam was the first created man in all of human history, and because of this fact, he served as the "head of humanity" (or the "federal head"). Since he alone held this position, most Protestant and Catholic teaching holds that all of humanity inherits his type of physical/spiritual existence, as well as the effects of his decisions. Namely, we inherit a fallen condition and a fallen world. By calling Jesus the "second Adam," Paul is making a very bold assertion—Jesus represents the dawn of a new creation; he is a new type of man. With this view, it seems as though Paul certainly saw himself as one who lives in the dawn of a new age:[26] an age that would ultimately give rise to a time when all believers would exist with the type of body the resurrected Jesus possesses. This is not to say that Jesus did not truly live as one of us—a life complete with all of the trials and temptations of our earthly existence. Rather, it says something about the *present* existence of Jesus.

Paul was saying that while the resurrected Jesus is a new type of man, he *still* represents humanity in bodily form. He does so because he has replaced Adam as the head of humanity. This should have meant to the Corinthians that their Lord and Savior, the one to whom they had ultimately given their lives, was raised from the dead and transformed into a spiritual, and yes, *bodily* existence. The takeaway from this analogy is that Paul was explicitly saying that the physical component of life (the body) is not subordinate to our immaterial component (the soul).[27] If Christ himself was raised from the dead with a tangible body, then it only stands to reason that we will be too. This seems to be the heart of the issue that Paul was addressing in this chapter.

Paul's point would have been crystal clear to those who were hearing the letter read aloud in Corinth: believers have not already been given a heavenly existence (as some proposed), nor should we await a time when the soul is "liberated" from the physical body (as others proposed). Instead, believers are

---

[26] Ciampa and Rosner, "The Structure and Argument of 1 Corinthians: A Biblical/Jewish Approach," 66.

[27] George R. Beasley Murray, *New International Bible Commentary*, 153.

anxiously anticipating the time when our bodily existence will be like that of Jesus' rather than Adam's. *Life as a disembodied spirit is not the hope of Christianity. Rather, a perfected, bodily existence is the hope.* While many scholars would agree on this point, I diverge with the common view about one very important thing: I believe Paul was saying that a conscious, disembodied existence will not be realized at any point. We never consciously exist without a body.

The previous points lend themselves to Paul's greater eschatological—which is a fancy word for how the end of the age and God's plans will all work out—view, which is extremely pronounced here in 1 Corinthians 15. There can be no doubt that the resurrection of Jesus was the centerpiece of Paul's ministry and his eschatological view. This truth becomes plain throughout the chapter, as Paul hangs the entirety of the faith on this historical event. If the Resurrection did not happen, then Paul and the apostles had misinterpreted God by affirming the event (15:15). If the Resurrection had not occurred, then the proclamation and the faith it has produced is absolutely meaningless (15:16). Paul went so far as to say that Christians should be pitied if there is no resurrection (15:19). In 15:35-49, Paul was not only telling the church in Corinth about his doctrine of the resurrection, but was also telling them about the event that holds every other article of faith together. Biblical scholar Gordon Fee has summarized Paul's view on the subject admirably: "Everything is up for grabs—Christ's death as a saving event, forgiveness of sins, hope for the future, Christian ethics, the character of God Himself—if there is no resurrection."[28] Without this event, there would be no need for letters, moral discipline, theological discussion, or even faith itself.

Whether it does so directly or indirectly, this text shapes the way that nearly all of the other passages about the state of the dead should be viewed. The reason is that it tells us a great deal about the nature of the relationship between the body and the soul. Of the one hundred and forty-two times that the Greek word *soma* (meaning "body") or one of its variants is used within the New Testament, roughly one-fourth of them are found within the two letters to the Corinthians.[29] Paul used this term nine times in 1 Corinthians 15:35-44 alone. As most of us know, the repetition of specific words and themes suggests an emphasis in thought; Paul was really trying to tell them something! Paul's entire point about the nature of the resurrection in chapter

---

[28] Gordon P. Fee, *The New Interpretive Commentary on the New Testament: The First Epistle to the Corinthians*, 775.
[29] *Strong's Greek Concordance*, BibleHub.

15 is of dire importance within our discussion about the state of the dead. In no uncertain terms, *Paul was saying that a substantive body is not only important, but critically necessary*. This is true of how we presently live, how Christ lived (and lives), and how we will one day live when Christ returns. Paul's opponents in Corinth failed to understand this point. Unfortunately, so have many well-intentioned Christians.

Clearly, God desired that we have physical bodies from the beginning. To go even further with Paul's view in this chapter, his argument is that substantive bodies are not just natural and intended during this lifetime, but also in the next (15:49). Paul made a specific point to deny the idea that human beings possess a soul that is wholly separable from the body, much less one that can "fly off" and live somewhere on its own. New Testament scholar Ben Witherington III has pointed out that the Greek term we often translate as "soul" (*psuche*) is essentially the "life breath" that was given to Adam (and all human beings) at creation.[30] The earlier Hebrew word we often translate as "soul" (*nepes*) carries with it the same essential meaning, and is most literally speaking of the entire person or being.[31] Both of these observations are incredibly important. A living, conscious human being consists of both a body and a soul, and that will not even change at the resurrection. The early Christian apologist Justin Martyr expressed the very same sentiment in the second century AD:

> "Is the soul by itself man? No; but the soul of man. Would the body be called man? No, but it is called the body of man. If, then, neither of these is by itself man, but that which is made up of the two together is called man, and God has called man to life and resurrection, He has called not a part, but the whole, which is the soul and the body."[32]

True to the Jewish teachings of the Old Testament, Paul did not intend that the body and soul should be viewed as two separate entities that can exist apart from one another. In general, this view seemed to be the one at play with Paul's opponents in Corinth. As I explain in chapter four, I view the soul as a quality that emerges from (or with) the physical body rather than as a being of its own: as something like information, really. Overall, it

---

[30] Ben Witherington III, *Revelation and the End Times*, 65.

[31] *Mounce's Complete Expository Dictionary of Old and New Testament Words*, 670-71.

[32] Justin Martyr, *On the Resurrection*, chapter 8.

is clear that the continuity between the body and the soul is intrinsic within the Jewish mindset about the "soul."[33] By extension, the traditional Jewish (and *early* Christian) perspective on this relationship is rather straightforward: "The belief that the soul continues its existence after the dissolution of the body is a matter of philosophical or theological speculation rather than of simple faith, and is accordingly nowhere expressly taught in Holy Scripture."[34]

The relationship between the body and the soul can be likened to the workings of a clock; the minute hand and the hour hand operate together simultaneously. While they each serve a different purpose, and are not identical—the minute hand is not the hour hand, and vice versa—neither part can tell time on its own. This analogy displays the very thing that separates the person you see in a casket from the one you once interacted with in life—the body and the soul are no longer united. The life force has left the person, and so the body and soul are no longer united. However, the soul does not emerge as its own being at that point. I do not take the inextricable continuity of the body and soul to mean that the soul is the "spark of life" or the "animating quality of the body," as it is often proposed to be. The Spirit of God— "the Lord and giver of life," as the Nicene Creed puts it—is the source of life. This life was breathed into Adam (man) at creation, and flows to all who have come after him. The Spirit, not the human soul, is what makes us alive. I believe that the soul is the quality that stores our personal information (our identities). This identity is both indissolubly bound to, and shaped by, the body and the material world. In a very real sense, one might refer to the soul as "identity information." The soul is the information of our earthly lives.

I believe this view of the body-soul relationship helps to make sense of the mystery that this life is somehow connected to the next. The body will be different, but the identity will not. Perhaps this is why Jesus' closest companions didn't *physically* recognize him after the Resurrection, but knew him only when he revealed elements of his character to them. I will return to this topic in much greater detail in chapter four, as it has much to tell us about

---

[33] Bemporad records that " . . . the most important Hebrew words for this concept (*nefesh, neshamah* or *nishmah*, and *ruah*) do not primarily refer to appearance, destiny, power, or supernatural influences, but to respiration—the inner, animating element of life." The point being here that the soul was not understood as something detachable from the human body. The language simply doesn't allow that. "Soul: Jewish Concept."

[34] "Immortality of the Soul," JewishEncyclopedia.com.

our own lives after death. For the time being, the central point is that Paul's teachings here in 1 Corinthians reveal to us that bodies and souls cannot consciously live apart from one another. The separation of the body and the soul is a result of death, not some entrance into a different type of life. More than that, neither the body nor the soul constitutes a "living being" in and of itself; both are necessary for human existence, whether we are talking about this life or the next. Jesus' resurrection is living proof of that fact.

With all that I have previously evaluated, it seems extraordinarily unlikely that Paul envisioned slipping out of his body to live as a disembodied spirit in heaven or some temporary holding place. It appears that the immortal classic, "I'll Fly Away," got it wrong, at least on this front. To counteract the threat of those who insisted that the incorporeal soul was superior to the earthly body, Paul wrote this entire chapter (15). But who, exactly, was attempting to convince the believers in Corinth that the body is of lesser value than the soul? While Greek philosophical beliefs about the soul were extremely prevalent (and diverse), the presence of at least early Gnostic thought in Corinth has been documented for quite some time now.[35] The Gnostics were, no doubt, heavily influenced by Greek philosophy, particularly the Platonic variety. While there were many varieties of Gnosticism, most Gnostics viewed the human body, and even the physical world we inhabit, as being a hindrance to humanity's true nature.[36]

Though many Gnostics viewed the physical body as an evil (or at least, an inferior) tomb that restricts our much more desirable spirit from flying away to the heavens, Paul was absolutely insistent that no such thing will *ever* actually take place. Jesus proved the point by conquering death through the reception of a resurrection body; he never so much as appeared to anyone as an immaterial spirit. Likewise, believers will certainly reign with Christ at his return, but not as immaterial beings. It appears that the more "traditional" Christian views of the afterlife do not match up with the teachings of Scripture. But they do align with the teachings of the Gnostics.

If Paul's opponents in Corinth were indeed correct, then his entire case to the Corinthians is rendered both useless and hypocritical. Paul's opponents would have been correct in their assessment of the body-soul relationship, and

---

[35] For more information about the Gnostic influence in Corinth, refer to Schmithals' and Steely's, *Gnosticism in Corinth*.

[36] G.L Borchert, "Gnosticism," in the *Evangelical Dictionary of Biblical Theology*, 485-488.

Paul would have wasted a tremendous amount of time refuting a perspective that he ultimately agreed with. This is crucial. It is this point that must be factored into our assessment of any text that discusses the afterlife. This is particularly, but by no means exclusively, true of those occasions where Paul discussed the matter. This basic understanding of the relationship between the body and the soul serves as the first of two foundational elements within my view of the state of the dead and the afterlife. This most definitely does not mean that it somehow stands outside the bounds of the rest of the biblical testimony. As we will see, the sum of the scriptural evidence is completely consistent with Paul's message to the church at Corinth. One such example of this consistency is found in Paul's first letter to the Thessalonians, which contains the second of my foundational texts. We now turn to this passage.

DON'T FORGET DESSERT: 1 THESSALONIANS 4:13-18

Contrary to what many skeptics and nonbelievers might say, the Bible is one of the most complex and sophisticated pieces of literature in existence. It is not some foolish text that was written by ignorant peasants or intellectually simple folk. While the essential messages are clear enough for all to understand, parts of the Bible can go deeper than we are able to follow. Though many topics within its pages can be easily discerned, others can be almost impossible to perfectly decipher. Within this, there is certainly room for differing interpretations concerning a variety of biblical issues. What are we to make of the divine execution of Ananias and Sapphira in Acts 5? How is it that the sun and moon were not created until the fourth day within the Genesis account (1:14-19), when "days" were said to exist before that? Further, there is yet another list of topics that the Bible doesn't really address at all. How, for example, should we feel about the social and moral implications of selecting political candidates? Can we really just pretend that we can vote for candidates without regard for the decisions they will make if elected? Or, what should we do when a group of miscreants attempts to harm us and our families? Should we let them rape our wives and daughters, and torture our sons (yes, this happens)? Is that really what Jesus meant when he said, "turn the other cheek"? If it isn't—*and I firmly believe that it isn't*— how exactly are we to handle these types of situations?

Looking elsewhere, how do we decide the exact laws that transition from God's covenant with Israel (the first) to the covenant made with all who believe in Christ (the second)? While the New Testament does not specifically condemn things like rape or pedophilia, you should never hear a sermon in defense of either practice. We assume (and rightfully so) that these types of laws logically transition into the new covenant. Here is the point: whether we like it or not, there are issues within the Bible that are not obviously spelled out, and there are a host of others that are neither black and white nor clear as crystal. So before moving on to issues and passages that are very much open to interpretation— "grey areas," if you will—this passage in 1 Thessalonians starts us out with something that is much more theologically discernible. I am speaking here of the way we are instructed to view our greatest enemy— death. Perhaps no other issue better illustrates the human struggle after the Fall than the reality of death.

Of all the ways that the biblical authors could have described the nature of death, the analogy of choice was the one between *death* and *sleep*. What was death like to those who authored our biblical texts? Apparently, it is more similar to bedtime than anything else they could imagine. If you believe that the Bible is the inspired word of God that has been revealed to us through human authors—in any capacity—then sleep is evidently the way that God wants us to think of death as well. While Paul was not the first biblical author to use this comparison—the prophet Daniel did so hundreds of years before Saul of Tarsus was even a thought (Dan. 12:1-4), for example—he was certainly its most prolific supporter. But how did Paul view the correlation between death and sleep in his own writings? In order to answer that question, we turn to Paul's most thorough explanation of the matter: 1 Thessalonians 4:13-18.

> "Brothers and sisters, we do not want you to be uninformed about those who sleep in death, so that you do not grieve like the rest of mankind, who have no hope. For we believe that Jesus died and rose again, and so we believe that God will bring with Jesus those who have fallen asleep in him. According to the Lord's word, we tell you that we who are still alive, who are left until the coming of the Lord, will certainly not precede those who have fallen asleep. For the Lord himself will come down from heaven, with a loud command, with the voice of the archangel and with the trumpet call of God, and the dead in Christ will rise first. After that, we who are still alive and are left will be caught

up together with them in the clouds to meet the Lord in the air. And so we will be with the Lord forever. Therefore encourage one another with these words."

If 1 Corinthians 15:35-58 is Paul's *tour de force* on the nature of the resurrection, then 1 Thessalonians 4:13-18 serves an equivalent role concerning the Parousia (the second "coming" of Christ). If you have ever been to a funeral, you may well remember hearing this passage read aloud during the service, as it speaks directly to the issue of death. This passage succinctly states the way that Paul perceived the events of Christ's return, the order of the resurrection, and the nature of the interim period (again, the period between death and resurrection). But before moving on to the meat of the text, it is worth mentioning that the overall discussion we are evaluating here between Paul and the church at Thessaloniki would have provided the perfect opportunity to talk about "dying and going to heaven," or anything of the sort. The believers in that particular church were, like many of us, very concerned about what would happen to those who had passed away before the return of Christ. If Paul's perspective was that the human soul would enter into a conscious existence elsewhere after the death of the body, then it is worth wondering why he took such pains *not* to say that. Paul could very easily have said something like this:

> "But we do not want you to be uninformed, brothers, about those who *have died*, that you may not grieve as others do who have no hope. *For we know that those who have died in Christ are already present with him, enjoying the heavenly existence that was promised to us.*"

Clearly, the words in italics are my own and not Paul's, but any statement of the sort would have clarified that the dead consciously reside in heaven (or elsewhere). I would suggest that if Paul had said such a thing, whether in this passage or another, then there would be no need to debate the nature of the interim period at all. But instead of attempting to discuss the dead in any sort of conscious way, Paul compared death to sleep. Moreover, Paul placed the entire basis of our hope in the afterlife in the future: at the return of Christ. It strikes me as odd that when the opportunity presented itself—and again, presented itself *perfectly*—to affirm that believers enjoy a conscious, heavenly existence at death, Paul clearly chose to go a different direction. If he believed that, he really blew the opportunity to say it! I realize that this particular objection will not satisfy some readers, and I will now base my arguments on what Paul chose to say rather than what he chose not to say. Nevertheless, it is certainly worth remembering that Paul was unwilling to openly state that the souls of the dead enter into a conscious existence after death, even when the opportunity to do so was slapping him in the face.

Within this passage, the word "sleep" (*koimaomai*) is used on three separate occasions. Clearly, this term is intended to be synonymous with the word "dead," which is used in verse 16. We can look at Jesus' explanation of Lazarus' condition in John 11:11 for another example of this particular analogy, but the theme is consistent throughout the Bible.[37] Without question, those who are "asleep" are those who have died. To be very clear here, *sleep = death* within this analogy. So far, this much is irrefutable—Paul certainly believed that being dead was in some way similar to being asleep. The question being begged, of course, is this: in what way are these two concepts actually related? When we evaluate this connection, even at the surface-level, it isn't overly difficult to see the possibilities. For starters, the sleep-death comparison works well because every single human being that has ever walked the face of the earth either has died or will die (save for Elijah and Enoch, anyway). Unless one belongs to the generation of people who will be alive to witness the return of Christ, everyone sleeps and everyone dies. While this association is certainly true, we cannot help but wonder if there isn't more to the story. Is the certainty of death and sleep the extent to which Paul envisioned the comparison?

If the association were only true insomuch as both events come part and parcel with being human, then it is reasonable to conclude that Paul could have used any number of analogies besides sleep. Why, then, did Paul choose to compare death to sleep? Three very important clues are revealed when we simply consider what happens when we sleep. First and foremost, we are not conscious when we sleep. While one could insert a number of synonyms for the term *conscious*—like "alert," "mindful," "aware," or even "awake"—the fact remains that being asleep is precisely when we as human beings are *unconscious*. We are not capable of knowing what is going on in the world around us—say, our bedrooms—while we are asleep. This, of course, is why we are often anesthetized during surgery. If we were aware of

---

[37] See Daniel 12:2, John 11:11-14, Acts 7:60, and 1 Corinthians 15:6; 18, 20, 51, for some examples.

our surroundings or able to know what is happening to us while we sleep, then we would not actually be asleep. Therefore, if we are not unconscious while we are asleep (or knocked out, in a coma, etc.), then under what other circumstance could we be described as being unconscious? Yes, we are indeed unconscious when we are asleep.

The second key aspect about sleep is logically connected to the first, and it has to do with time. While we are asleep, we have no concept of time. Certainly, we can wake up to use the bathroom in the middle of the night and once again become aware of how much time has elapsed since we laid down for bed. While we are asleep, however, we are not capable of understanding the passing of hours and minutes, nor are we even able to feel ordinary human sensations (like bladder pain or discomfort). This is why we set alarms and order wake-up calls. This is also why people who awake from comas—however long or short they may be—have no idea how much time has passed.

The final reality of sleep was perhaps the most crucial in Paul's mind, and it is the fact that sleep is a temporary condition. Whether we fall asleep, enter into a coma, or become unconscious by some other means, it could never be a permanent state of existence. Ultimately, we will either wake up or pass away, and there is no other option available to us. So, now we have our three significant discoveries concerning sleep: we are *unconscious*, we have *no concept of time*, and we are only *temporarily* in this state of being. Perhaps this is more along the lines of what Paul imagined when he chose to compare death to sleep rather than to something like digestion.

With these aspects in mind, the ramifications of the sleep-death analogy should be very profound. In Paul's view, death presents a time when we are completely unaware of the comings and goings of this world (or any other). This is good reason to take something like Jesus' parable of the Rich Man and Lazarus as an actual parable (which I later evaluate in detail), being that it would otherwise portray that we are somehow conscious in death. Qohelet appears to have gotten this one right as well, when he said that "the dead know nothing."[38] This leads quite naturally to the point that we have no concept of time in death, either. As far as we are concerned, absolutely no time will have passed from the moment we take our final breaths to the day when Jesus has returned and the judgment is at hand. As difficult as that is to imagine, it is the ultimate conclusion of this type of prolonged "sleep."

This is exactly why a text like Philippians 1:23 can make sense in two

---

[38] Ecclesiastes 9:5.

different ways—we could immediately depart to be with Christ, *or* we could wait a million years to do so. Either way, we would never know the difference; to "depart" *is* to directly be with Christ, as far as the departed understand things. The final piece of the puzzle is that death, like sleep, is not a permanent state of being. In Paul's writings, the very thing that separates Christians from the non-believing world concerning death is that we know we will conquer it:

> "Brothers and sisters, we do not want you to be uninformed about those who sleep in death, *so that you do not grieve like the rest of mankind, who have no hope.* For we believe that Jesus died and rose again, and so we believe that God will bring with Jesus those who have fallen asleep in him."[39]

To the Christian, death is not the end of the story. Instead, it is but a pause between this earthly existence and the everlasting Kingdom that is coming.

To this point, I have evaluated the distinct correlations between the properties of sleep and the properties of death. The most common objection concerning these principles is that the sleep comparison was intended to describe the body and not the soul.[40] This is incorrect for two major reasons. The first is that the "natural body" (as Paul called it) will not be reused after death, so it's not awaiting anything. How can something be reused if it no longer exists? This is true of every deceased human body, given enough time. The second reason this objection fails is that the body cannot do anything, like sleep, in death. A soul cannot do so either, which is why the term "soul sleep" (discussed later) fails to convey the appropriate message. To speak of either the body or the soul as being "asleep" is to create a drastic separation between them; it is to make them into two different beings, of sorts. For this reason, the sleep comparison was used to describe *the entire being* rather than either the body or the soul separately. When we are dead, the entire person is "asleep" and unconscious, not just the body.

To recap, I have made the case that death can be compared to sleep for three specific reasons:

1) Both are unconscious modes of existence.
2) Both are characterized by the absence of temporal recognition.

---

[39] 1 Thessalonians 4:13-14 (emphasis mine).

[40] Moreland and Habermas make this case, as does N.T. Wright. See *Beyond Death*, 228, and *Surprised by Hope*, 171.

3) Both are merely temporary in nature.

But if this is accurate, one very important question remains—when do we "wake up" from our slumber? You may have heard that a verse like Philippians 1:23 again provides us with the answer; we wake up immediately after we die! We would have to, right, since "Christ will bring with him those who have fallen asleep" (1 Thes. 4:14)? In order to bring believers back to earth, it seems logically necessary to assume that believers will be with Christ prior to his arrival. Put another way, you cannot bring something with you that is not already in your possession.

While this line of reasoning appears to make a great deal of sense, it is also incomplete because verse 4:14 must be interpreted within the context of the entire passage. This failure to evaluate the scriptural message (or even individual passages) *as a whole* is usually the fatal flaw in any doctrine that affirms a conscious intermediate existence. I will later divulge this type of misunderstanding within some of the popular interpretations of the Rich Man and Lazarus, as well as within the story of the Witch of Endor, and Jesus' conversation with the criminal on the cross. All of these accounts can lead us to believe in immediate, continued consciousness after death, if we fail to evaluate the entire passages. Like these examples, this passage in 1 Thessalonians tells a very different story when we evaluate it in its entirety. Certainly, we should all agree that fallen believers are said to be returning with Christ at his coming. The exact time that deceased believers first join Christ before his return is the pivotal point, however. Fortunately, Paul clarifies this for us in verses 15-18:

> ". . . we who are still alive, who are left until the coming of
> the Lord, will certainly not precede those who have fallen
> asleep. For the Lord himself will come down from heaven,
> with a loud command, with the voice of the archangel and
> with the trumpet call of God, and the dead in Christ will
> rise first."

When will the dead be raised to meet Christ? According to Paul, it will happen when the Lord returns from heaven and calls out to *wake them up*. Not before, and not after. When last I checked, Jesus has not returned, and no earth-shattering noises have erupted to wake the dead. Did I miss it?

After the dead have been raised during Christ's return, Paul indicates to us what will become of those believers who are alive on earth at that time: "Then we who are alive, who are left, will be caught up together with them in the clouds to meet the Lord in the air, and so we will always be with the Lord" (v. 17). By including *the rest of the passage*, Paul's vision of Christ's return and the state of the dead becomes much clearer. Rather than asserting that we die and immediately enter into glory as disembodied spirits, we now see that all of this occurs at the point when the Kingdom comes in its fullness: when heaven fully merges with earth in a remade creation. This is why I am insistent that we view this entire issue in the same way that Paul did: *eschatologically*—meaning the way all of this ends up working out—rather than *proximally*. The biblical authors saw the resurrection, the judgment, and everlasting life as issues that will all be wrapped up together at the end of the age when Jesus returns.

The order of things, then, sounds something like this: Jesus returns to earth, the "trumpet" blasts, the dead awake from their metaphorical slumber to join Jesus as he returns from the heavens, and then his living followers are "caught up" (*raptured*, as many unfortunately call it) to cap off his triumphant return. This means that deceased believers actually do come with Christ at his return, but this is only true because Jesus is going to raise them *during* his return to our world. At such a point, the soul (the identity information, as I later explain) that God has been storing will be united with a body fit for the new age. This is what resurrection means in the eschatological sense. It is not a matter of actually pulling dead bodies out of the earth, but of creating new ones. The difference between Christ's body and that of someone like Lazarus is that his had been perfected; Christ did not come back as he was, but as he (and someday, *we*) will always be. This is consistent with Paul's words in 1 Corinthians 15:51-52: "Listen, I tell you a mystery: We will not all sleep, but we will all be changed—in a flash, in the twinkling of an eye, at the last trumpet. For the trumpet will sound, the dead will be raised imperishable, and we will be changed."

While I believe this point can stand on its own, the problem it poses to the TDP (*temporary-disembodiment position*) compounds when we consider who is actually supposed to be with Christ at the onset of his return. There is more than sufficient biblical evidence to suggest that the angels are the only beings to hold such a position. 2 Thessalonians 1:5-10 tells us that the angels will be with Christ when he is revealed from heaven, on "the day he comes to be glorified." Jude 14 says that the Lord will come with "thousands upon thousands of his holy ones" to judge the ungodly. Though the expression

24

"holy ones" (*hagiais*) does not directly reveal the identity of these beings, it is almost certainly a reference to the angels. Jesus made this point abundantly clear in Mark 8:38: "If anyone is ashamed of me and my words in this adulterous and sinful generation, the Son of Man will be ashamed of them when he comes in his Father's glory with the holy angels." We see exactly the same point about the angels in Matthew 25:31 and 16:27, and within the Parable of the Weeds (Mt. 13:24-43).

Within all of these references, there is no mention of deceased believers existing with Christ at the beginning of the Parousia (the second "coming"); only the angels are discussed in this way. While some believe that we are turned into angels when we die, that belief doesn't pass muster either. The TDP recognizes that we exist only as disembodied spirits until the general resurrection, and we are not changed into angelic form until that time.[41] Further, these passages reveal that one of the most essential purposes of Christ's return is, as the Nicene Creed puts it, "to judge the quick and the dead."[42] How can Christ come back to judge the dead, if the (righteous) dead are already with him in heaven? This would of course require multiple judgments, a concept that is nowhere spoken of in Scripture.[43]

One might point to a text like Hebrews 12:22-23,[44] but this is not an allusion to naked spirits who presently live with Christ. Like the rest of the passage, both the present and future realities are blended together to express the superiority of the second covenant. This is a vision of all the hopes that are brought forth within the new covenant. It directly mentions that our *names* are written in heaven, and the subsequent reference to the "spirits of the righteous made perfect" is probably an allusion to those believers who were still alive: those who had already been purified through faith. Revelation 6:9-11 is wielded as similar "evidence" about believers reigning with Christ. This text falls right within one of the most illustrative and metaphorical sections of the entire Bible. While most people do not even attempt to explain the true meaning of any of the "seven seals" or take them at face value, some are

---

[41] See the section entitled, "It's All Substantive," in chapter four.

[42] "The Nicene Creed."

[43] See chapter four's section, "What God Has Put Asunder, Let No Man Join Together," for a more detailed description of this particular problem.

[44] "But you have come to Mount Zion, to the city of the living God, the heavenly Jerusalem. You have come to thousands upon thousands of angels in joyful assembly, to the church for the firstborn, whose names are written in heaven. You have come to God, the Judge of all, to the spirits of the righteous made perfect . . ."

more than eager to take the fifth one as a literal statement about where and how the dead presently exist. I hope the selective nature of this particular claim is apparent. We cannot view all of the other visions as being figurative but choose to take the fifth one as being stringently literal. This being said, the previous objection about Christ returning to judge both the living and the dead remains intact. I will return to this issue later on, but let's be clear about something: *the angels* are the only beings who are concretely mentioned as presently dwelling with God or returning with Christ, and dead people—regardless of what option we take on the afterlife—are not angels.

The question I posed at the onset of this section was this: can you bring something with you that you do not already possess? In this scenario, it appears that such a thing is not only possible, but is exactly what Paul had in mind. As strange as it sounds, we can actually compare this amazing event to an ordinary trip to the supermarket. Imagine that a friend has invited you to dinner, and has asked you to bring the dessert. While you do not presently have this dessert with you, not to worry—you can stop at the local market *on the way there* and purchase it. When you later arrive at your friend's gathering, it would then be accurate to say that *you have brought the dessert with you*. Apparently, this is what will happen at the world's most incredible dinner party—the great Wedding Feast of the Lamb (Rev. 19:6-9). In keeping with our supermarket analogy, Jesus (with his angels) will stop and "pick up" those who have died while on route to meet the living. During this process, Christ's return and the reception of our resurrection bodies occur simultaneously. The dead *are* returning with Jesus, but they were not previously living with him in a conscious state of being.

At this point, one might suggest that there are two options within this analogy. While it is true that you could pick up dessert on the way, you could also simply have the dessert with you already: the "dessert," of course, being a reference to deceased believers. But this misses the point. My purpose here is to show that the passage—and the entire state of the dead discussion—makes the best sense if we opt for the view that Christ will resurrect believers and bring them back to earth with him in one major event. The dead are not consciously living with Christ (or living anywhere) at the present. I believe this explanation makes the best possible sense of the entire passage in 1 Thessalonians.

Thus, our quest to understand the comparison between sleep and death has come full circle. The result is a very plausible reason to believe that death represents a temporary period of unconsciousness—a time of "sleeping in"— until the day comes that Christ himself awakens us. All else aside, what sense would any of this make if the dead are not really dead? If the dead are already living as disembodied spirits, then Paul's words within 1 Thessalonians 4:13-18 simply do not make any sense. You cannot wake someone up who is already conscious, and you certainly cannot bring someone back to life who is already living.

As we begin to move towards passages that are used as evidence for the TDP (meaning the *temporary-disembodiment position*, as a reminder)—which are, by my estimation, much more debatable than Paul's message here in 1 Thessalonians—try to keep in mind the two critical teachings we have evaluated thus far. Based on 1 Corinthians 15, Paul revealed that the body and the soul are inextricably bound together. That is, if we are talking about living, breathing, functioning beings. In principle, a human soul is not capable of consciously living by itself, and there is good reason to believe that even the "next world" will be substantive in nature.[45] Additionally, our study of 1 Thessalonians 4:13-18 revealed that Paul's view of death was anything but the continuation of conscious existence. If it were, there is simply no reason why he should compare death to sleep rather than just affirming that the dead are presently enjoying the splendors of heaven (or someplace else). Now, with the basis of my belief in an unconscious state of the dead in place, we are prepared to move on to evaluating the biblical evidence used in favor of the TDP and any other view that suggests we will live as disembodied souls during the interim period. We will begin the next part of our journey in God's realm: heaven.

---

[45] See the section entitled, "It's All Substantive," in chapter four, for more details on this perspective.

CHAPTER TWO

OFF TO HEAVEN

Every beginning has an end, and every story a conclusion. So it is with the crowned jewel of God's creation—humanity. During our time on earth, the normal person experiences his or her fair share of good times and bad times, highs and lows, and peaks and valleys. The latter of each pairing is of course what makes life so very difficult. To anyone who has seen a loved one die or has seriously faced his or her own mortality, it is apparent that perhaps nothing is harder to deal with or is more terrifying than the certainty that we will one day perish from the earth. In the meantime, we are forced to watch those around us transition from our lives to our memories. Thankfully, all Bible-believing Christians are united in the common belief that death is not the end of the story. Just as Christ was raised from the dead, so shall we be (2 Cor. 4:14). Indeed, the Christian faith holds that all believers will one day fully inherit the Kingdom of God with Christ himself (Rom. 8:17).

On the other hand, the Bible also holds that those who reject God and choose to follow the powers of darkness will ultimately end up in a place called "hell." At the beginning of the fourth chapter, I will discuss this realm of existence and what it can actually tell us about the state of the dead. Throughout this particular chapter, I will evaluate much of the biblical evidence used to describe an intermediate existence in heaven. The specific task will be to assess whether or not this information is actually consistent with the most common Christian beliefs about the afterlife. To state the question very clearly: do believers really go directly to heaven after death? To answer this question, we turn once more to the apostle Paul.

BODY AND FLESH

In this section, I will begin to evaluate a series of biblical passages that are commonly used to support the belief that Christians die and go to heaven as disembodied spirits/souls. Though they are few in number, they are often considered to be strong in substance. Not surprisingly, there are certain key features that all of these passages share. Most specifically, they all seem to imply that life away from this body (in death) means life with Christ (in heaven). As I assess these passages, I ask that you enter into this section with an open mind. My case is relatively straightforward: while these references certainly *can be* viewed as evidence that the soul consciously departs to heaven at death, there is more than sufficient reason to reject that interpretation. This is particularly true when these passages are not viewed in isolation, but viewed in light of the entire canon of Scripture. I will begin by addressing Paul's words in Philippians 1:22-24, which is easily one of the most quoted passages in the entire Bible concerning the state of the dead:

> "If I am to live in the flesh, that means fruitful labor for me; and I do not know which I prefer. I am hard pressed between the two: my desire is to depart and be with Christ, for that is far better; but to remain in the flesh is more necessary for you."

Admittedly, this passage serves as one of the most convincing pieces of evidence in favor of the TDP. When verse 23 is taken at a surface-level reading, it seems almost overwhelming: ". . . my desire is to depart and be with Christ, for that is far better." When several factors are considered, however, the statement becomes more ambiguous. One oddity of this passage is that Paul opted not to use the Greek word *soma* (body) to explain his perspective. This is particularly strange when we consider that Paul used this word in a very similar discussion in 2 Corinthians 5:1-10 (discussed below). Again, *soma* refers very strictly to a tangible body, which was crucial in our evaluation of 1 Corinthians 15. But instead of using *soma*, Paul used the more theologically-loaded term *sarx*. This may prove to have been most intentional.

The word *sarx* (translated as "flesh") is a relatively common term within the writings of the New Testament, where it is used nearly one hundred and fifty times.[46] This word can have very special significance, particularly in Paul's writings. To Paul, the "flesh" was more than just the material nature of our reality. He certainly used the word *sarx* to talk about the physical structure that covers our muscles and bones (1 Cor. 15:39), but he often used it to discuss the overall reality of life in a fallen world and the possession of a tarnished human nature (Rom. 8:13). In Paul's mind, this is also the current state of the entire creation (Rom. 8:22). In this sense, "flesh" refers to the entirety of our current state of being and our fallen existence. In other words, everything that human beings negatively experience would be considered in context. Sickness, frailty, the certainty of death, and the reality of living in a corrupted world; all of this would factor into the discussion.

This understanding of *sarx* is displayed quite well in Galatians 5:16-17: "Live by the Spirit, I say, and do not gratify the desires of the flesh. For what the flesh desires is opposed to the Spirit, and what the Spirit desires is opposed to the flesh." Paul could not have been saying that our physical "flesh" is opposed to the Spirit of God; God gave it to us, after all. Instead, it is clear that Paul's use of the word often refers to our fallen nature. This means that Paul's use of the phrase "remain in the flesh" could perhaps be viewed as being equivalent to something like "remain in this current state of being." This is the difference between life in the old age (the age of sin and death) and life in the new age (the age of righteousness and life).

With this understanding in place, the passage begins to make a little more sense. Paul was not envisioning the day he would leave his physical flesh and become a spirit in heaven. This would be a complete reversal of everything previously mentioned in 1 Corinthians 15, as well as a Gnostic-like misuse of the concept of the human soul. At the same time, he also didn't expect to be given his resurrection body yet, since that is irrefutably supposed to take place at Christ's coming. It appears that Paul was actually looking forward to leaving this entire mode of existence, and all that it entailed. When understood in this way, leaving the flesh certainly would be "better" because it is weak and corrupted. For those who think this sounds like "escapist" theology—which generally suggests that we should focus on dying and going to heaven in order to *escape* a world that is beyond all sense of help—this is nothing of the sort. Paul was deeply invested in helping to bring God's Kingdom to earth, just as we should be. The point is that Paul

---

[46] James A. Fowler, *"FLESH. What Does the Bible Mean by the Term 'flesh'?"*

had a very tough life as the apostle to the Gentiles, and that element must be factored into the discussion.

Paul personally admitted that he was forced to endure some type of ailment that made his work as an apostle more difficult (2 Cor. 12:7-10). As an interesting side note, the word Paul used when he referred to his "thorn in the *flesh*" is the same term he used in Philippians 1:22—*sarki*, a variant of the word *sarx*: the implication being that he desired to leave the existence that was so heavily flawed by his struggle. We must remember that Paul was getting to be an older man, and that he had been stoned, shipwrecked, beaten many times over, and severely malnourished throughout his years of ministry.[47] On top of all of that, it is likely that Paul wrote to the Philippians near (or during) the time of his first imprisonment in Rome. It is no stretch to say that Paul had suffered greatly by this point in his ministry, and was probably ready to reach the "goal" that he had long been running towards.[48] This is exactly the sentiment we later read about in 2 Timothy 4:6-8:

> "For I am already being poured out like a drink offering, and the time for my departure is near. I have fought the good fight, I have finished the race, I have kept the faith. Now there is in store for me the crown of righteousness, which the Lord, the righteous Judge, will award to me on that day—and not only to me, but also to all who have longed for his appearing."

Again, Paul echoes his sentiment that it would be more preferable to leave this mode of existence; the new Kingdom and the "crown of righteousness" awaited him. All of this is precisely why Paul told the believers in Philippi that it was better *for them* if he remained on this earth, but better *for him* if he didn't. The same could be said about a large number of believers throughout the ages. Tremendous suffering has often come part and parcel with following Christ. But notice also that Paul places the time when he would receive his crown at the very end of the age—on "that day" and at "his (Christ's) appearing"—rather than at the moment of death. Paul was consistent in his teachings, too. He applied the same reasoning about all believers in his letter to the Colossians when he said, "When Christ, who is your life, appears, then

---

[47] 2 Corinthians 11:16-29 tells of Paul's astonishing list of sufferings, many of which should have been fatal.

[48] Philippians 3:12-14.

you also will appear with him in glory" (3:4). These points are all the more reason why the typical understanding of Paul's words in Philippians 1:22-24 does not make sense of his overall position.

Though it could be argued that Paul would not have said that to depart and be with Christ is "better" unless he envisioned an immediate life of bliss in heaven, the previous points provide a very plausible alternative to that line of reasoning. For Paul, to leave a fallen body and a fallen world is to be ready to enter into an age in which a perfected body and a perfected world is the new reality, and he was ready for it. Furthermore, Paul's view of death as an existence which is comparable to sleep clarifies that "to depart and be with Christ" is a reality that is tied up in the greater hope that all Christians share, which is to participate in God's Kingdom when Christ returns.[49]

This leads naturally to what is perhaps the most important point to consider within this passage: Paul provided no details about *when* he expected to be with the Lord. It is clear that this would happen after he left the "flesh," but that is actually an extremely vague description from a temporal aspect. Was this immediately after, or at some more distant time after his death? Or, did he simply anticipate that he would *ultimately* be with the Lord, as all Christians will be at the resurrection? As far as Paul knew (or anyone knows), the next thing he would comprehend was life with Christ. The idea that he intended his statement to be taken in the ultimate sense goes best with Paul's entire perspective about what happens when we die. In fact, the remainder of the letter to the Philippians provides even further reason to take this approach. Again, we have to keep reading rather than isolating a verse or two!

In Paul's exhortation to the church that they should continue to stay firm in the faith, he offers that he would be able to "boast on the day of Christ" that his labor was not in vain (2:14-16). When talking about his own desires for the afterlife, Paul again says nothing about dying and going to heaven. Rather, he says, "I want to know Christ and the power of his resurrection and the fellowship of sharing in his sufferings, becoming like him in his death, and so, somehow to attain the resurrection from the dead" (3:10-11). Even more clearly, he later says, "But our citizenship is in heaven. And we await a Savior from there, the Lord Jesus Christ, who, by the power that enables him to bring everything under his control, will transform our lowly bodies so that they will be like his glorious body" (3:20-21).

---

[49] Refer back to the section entitled, "Don't Forget Dessert," in chapter one, for further discussion of this point.

The reality is that *every* other statement Paul made concerning the afterlife in his letter to the Philippians centered entirely upon Christ's return and the resurrection. If Paul meant that he expected to go live as a disembodied spirit by what he said in 1:22-24, then he would have contradicted that statement several times over throughout the rest of the letter. This is all the more reason why we should seriously doubt that 1:22-24 was intended to express the immediacy of conscious life with Christ after death. But this reality is only visible when we keep reading and make it a point to examine the entire context of the situation rather than a few verses. I cannot help but wonder how many biblical disagreements would utterly vanish if we were all willing to be open to whatever the text actually says, and if we read passages within their respective contexts.

When all of these factors are considered, it is more than reasonable to believe that Paul did not intend to say that conscious, disembodied existence with Christ is the immediate result of death. While the most popular way of interpreting this passage is in the immediate (and conscious) sense, there is nothing that necessitates this view. I would suggest that going to be with Christ—whether it occurs instantaneously in our reckoning of time or not—is "better" than living within this fallen world, particularly for those who have to endure tremendous suffering. For those who experience the inexpressible sorrows that so often occur within our fallen world, the present existence may not be preferable at all, and I see no problem with anyone who longs for the day when we will experience life with perfected bodies and a perfected creation. In fact, those very beliefs were central motivating factors within the early church. To prevent too much redundancy, I will save further explanation of this passage for the sections that follow. As we will continue to see, a conscious interim period is not consistent with Paul's other descriptions of the afterlife.

PAUL, THE TENTMAKER

To continue the discussion about Paul's view of the body, we find ourselves back in his letters to the church at Corinth. This time, we are dealing with something Paul wrote in his second letter to the rather muddled and disobedient church. 2 Corinthians 5:1-10 reads as follows:

"For we know that if the earthly tent we live in is destroyed, we have a building from God, an eternal house in heaven, not built by human hands. Meanwhile we groan, longing to be clothed instead with our heavenly dwelling, because when we are clothed, we will not be found naked. For while we are in this tent, we groan and are burdened, because we do not wish to be unclothed but to be clothed instead with our heavenly dwelling, so that what is mortal may be swallowed up by life. Now the one who has fashioned us for this very purpose is God, who has given us the Spirit as a deposit, guaranteeing what is to come. Therefore we are always confident and know that as long as we are at home in the body we are away from the Lord. For we live by faith, not by sight. We are confident, I say, and would prefer to be away from the body and at home with the Lord. So we make it our goal to please him, whether we are at home in the body or away from it. For we must all appear before the judgment seat of Christ, so that each of us may receive what is due us for the things done while in the body, whether good or bad."

Like Philippians 1:22-24, this passage is thought to provide solid evidence that the human soul continues to consciously exist in heaven after the body expires.

Notice that we are again dealing with Paul's perspectives about being *in* or *out* of the *body*. Though Paul reverses the order of the outcomes (and very strategically, I might add), he essentially repeats the only possible realities about our lives—we are either "at home in the body" and "away from the Lord" (v. 6), or we are "away from the body" and "at home with the Lord" (v. 7). Clearly, Paul viewed the latter as being the ideal situation (v.8). This passage is very straightforward to a number of interpreters. For many, it clarifies the entire debate about what happens when we die; if we are not here in this body, we are consciously present with Christ. Put another way, our souls go directly to heaven (where Christ is) when we leave this earthly life. While there are a number of biblical and logical arguments against such a view, which I later address, there are once again some difficulties presented within the passage itself.

In addition to being the most influential apostle in the world, Paul was also known to make a mean tent. Paul actually supported his ministry by making and selling tents (Acts 18:3), which were very commonly used by travelers and vendors in his day. This being the case, it isn't surprising to see that his common job spilled over into his higher calling (being the apostle to the Gentiles) in this passage. The word we commonly translate as "tent" (*skēnous*) can be viewed as another way that Paul describes our physical nature. For those who like to keep track of such things, that makes three different words we have seen Paul use in this way (body, flesh, and tent). The first part of this passage is almost entirely about the material component of our existence. Paul mentions that if our earthly tent is destroyed, ". . . we have a building from God, a house not made with hands, eternal in the heavens" (5:1). The temptation is to take this as an affirmation that if the body is destroyed, our immaterial component will consciously find shelter in heaven. However, it is more realistic that Paul was simply providing a powerful message of comfort. Though we may perish from the earth, we can rest assured that Christ has prepared for us an everlasting existence in his Kingdom.

As with the previous passage in Philippians, this need not be viewed as an immediate consequence of death. Paul further discusses the Christian hope in verses 2-4, saying:

> "Meanwhile we groan, longing to be clothed instead with
> our heavenly dwelling, because when we are clothed, we will
> not be found naked. For while we are in this tent, we groan
> and are burdened, because we do not wish to be unclothed
> but to be clothed instead with our heavenly dwelling, so that
> what is mortal may be swallowed up by life."

Our bodies being what they are, "we groan" to escape the burdens of a fallen existence. We should not, however, wish to escape substantive existence altogether. We do not wish to be "found naked" or "unclothed," as many early Gnostics and Platonists of the day were promoting, but instead we desire to have a *better bodily existence*—the spiritual body that Christ now possesses (1 Cor. 15:49).

While it could appear that Paul was promoting the possibility of existing in a purely immaterial form, this interpretation misses the point. Paul is not saying that bodily existence is simply preferable to immaterial (naked) existence, as though we could actually live without a body. Rather, he is saying that substantive life is always the ultimate hope and the only genuine mode of existence for those entering into everlasting life. Just as a tent is a temporary dwelling for the traveler, the earthly body is a temporary condition that points forward to the possession of a lasting home. In this case, that "lasting home" is the resurrection body. If one chooses to believe that the soul consciously survives on its own after death, then the resurrection body is relegated to being some type of "bonus" rather than a necessity. If life as an immaterial being is better, then why add the body at all? I expand upon this point in much greater detail in chapter four.[50]

Another major problem is that there is a particular assumption made here which was previously addressed concerning Philippians 1:23: the conjecture that Paul *must have* envisioned immediate departure to heaven. Like other good apocalyptic thinkers of his day, Paul viewed the time he was living in as the beginning of the end. With the work of Christ completed—except for the actions surrounding his return—the end-time events had already begun, as the old age was now giving way to the new. Though it certainly awaits its fulfillment, Paul believed that the Kingdom of God was already entering into the world. In this sense, the past, present, and future are not as temporally confined as we might think. Furthermore, Paul and the other members of the early church probably never imagined that Christ would wait several millennia (or more) to return. They did not recognize this until well after Christ's ascension, at least.

Apparently, the church later began to understand something that we now know to be the case: God's plans for the world would stretch far into the future (2 Pet. 3:3-9). This is crucial being that 2 Corinthians 5:1-10 is often thought to portray that Paul believed he would *instantaneously* enter heaven upon leaving his "tent." While this is certainly possible within the context, it is more probable that Paul was again speaking in purely eschatological terms. That is, Paul may have been saying that the next conscious existence he would experience would be "at home with the Lord." Beyond our prior assumptions, nothing within these phrases necessitates that we view it one way or the other. To be away from the "body," the "flesh," or the "tent," need only to imply that we are no longer living *this life*, in *this age*, and at *this time*.

This may well be what Paul intended when he said, "We are confident, I say, and would prefer to be away from the body and at home with the Lord" (5:8). In this, Paul could have been saying that we desire for this age—and

---

[50] See the sections entitled, "Just Add Body" and "Why Add Body," in chapter 4.

all of the fallen realities it entails—to completely give way to the new age. So, perhaps this is not at all about individual souls returning "home" to heaven at death, but is rather about the corporate hope of what all believers will one day experience: the Kingdom of God coming to us. This is the grand hope that is revealed in Revelation 21:1; "Then I saw 'a new heaven and a new earth,' for the first heaven and the first earth had passed away, and there was no longer any sea."

It is clear that 2 Corinthians 5:1-10 and Philippians 1:22-24 share many commonalities. Not surprisingly, I have made similar objections (thus far) to the typical interpretations of both passages. In both instances, the thought is that to leave this world is to live as a disembodied soul in heaven. As I have discussed, neither passage dictates that we understand them in this way. While Paul may have intended that believers view them in this manner, his overall approach to the subject makes that rather unlikely. Whatever Paul meant within these passages, he certainly didn't dispense with many details about the interim period. As theologian Oscar Cullman points out, "Nothing is said in the New Testament about the details of the interim conditions. We hear only this: we are nearer to God."[51]

That is precisely the point: being "nearer to God" does not necessitate consciousness on our parts. An unconscious soul would be every bit as near to God as a conscious one. This is particularly true if we were to stop thinking of the soul as a being that is trapped within a physical body and began to look at the soul as "identity information," as I promote. At death, we would all be "nearer to God" because the entire sum of our life experiences and our personalities would return to our Creator, where that data would be held on file until the resurrection. Further, we must remember that no perceivable time would pass between death and the resurrection according to this view. We die, and then we are with God in the new creation. To us, this would be instantaneous. *Instantaneous.* Is it not possible that this is what Paul really meant?

For all of the reasons previously mentioned, as well as the ones to come, it is my opinion that the soul does not consciously persist anywhere or in any capacity prior to the resurrection. Hence, the question must now be raised: if we are not in this body, then where are we? This is where most of us have stopped our pursuits, and have assumed that we fluidly transition from this life to a heavenly, disembodied existence. Biblically speaking, however, we

---

[51] Oscar Cullmann, "Immortality of the Soul or Resurrection of the Dead?"

must find context for what such a passage actually means. The case is made throughout this book that immaterial consciousness is not possible apart from a physical body; a living being consists of both a body and a soul. Given the aforementioned options, this means that Paul was probably not making the case that being "at home with the Lord" was the instant result of being deceased. Rather, conscious existence with Christ is the *eventual* result of our deaths and our resurrections. With additional evaluation, we see that the text itself provides further reason to believe this.

By the time we reach the end of this passage in 2 Corinthians, Paul's concluding remarks end up being the most important ones (so far as we are presently concerned). Here, Paul says: "For we must all appear before the judgment seat of Christ, so that each of us may receive what is due us for the things done while in the body, whether good or bad" (5:10). While the thought that we will all face judgment is rather obvious within Christian teaching, the addition of the phrase "done while in the body" is not. Did you notice that Paul limited the judgment only to the things we do while living in this earthly condition? Put another way, we are only judged based on the lives we live in the here and now. Such a message is consistent with Jesus' parable of the Rich Man and Lazarus, which I discuss later. This at least means that we are not being assessed, in any way, for the things we would hypothetically do if we were to consciously exist somewhere else after death. For instance, nothing we would do at a place like Abraham's bosom counts towards the judgment that sends us to one of two everlasting destinations— God's Kingdom or hell.

This is particularly interesting when we consider that even the angels in heaven can make life-altering decisions (i.e. they have *choice*). The fall of Satan and his angels unequivocally proves this point. The place we *may* go, however, excludes the option of choice that is otherwise so crucial in God's dealings with the created beings. Are we to believe that the way we live during that time ceases to matter, or that it does not count towards the judgment? If we are conscious beings during the interim period, then it scarcely makes sense that it would operate in such a way. This passage urges us towards the understanding that we can only make judgment-worthy decisions during this lifetime. Being that Satan and his minions were able to make these types of choices—as fallen angelic beings who are *supposedly* immaterial—this is just further reason to believe that Paul was not envisioning a conscious, disembodied existence between this age and the next. This is quite the conundrum for those who believe in the TDP. But then again, the simplest answer may be the appropriate one. Perhaps we aren't actually conscious during the interim period at all, so we need not speculate as to what bearing our intermediate decisions would have on the judgment. Until the resurrection, life goes on for the living, but not for the dead. What an absurd proposition, I know: to suggest that the dead are actually . . . well, dead!

THERE AND BACK AGAIN: AN APOSTLE'S TALE

While the last two passages we looked at are often viewed as being sufficient evidence that the soul consciously survives at death, other passages are used to support this belief. Though I will later evaluate Jesus' use of the word "paradise" in the account of the criminal on the cross, he is not the only one to employ this term. In the next passage, Paul also uses this word to describe a very unique experience. We find this in 2 Corinthians 12:2-4, as part of an intriguing account of *someone's* trip to the "third heaven:"

> "I know a man in Christ who fourteen years ago was caught
> up to the third heaven. Whether it was in the body or out
> of the body I do not know—God knows. And I know that
> this man—whether in the body or apart from the body I do
> not know, but God knows—was caught up to paradise and
> heard inexpressible things, things that no one is permitted
> to tell."

One of the mysterious parts of this passage is the question of who Paul is referring to. While this issue could be a topic unto itself, it's not particularly crucial to the issue at hand. Overall, the case that Paul is actually referring to himself has been well-documented and makes a great deal of sense in context.[52] The important aspect of this passage, for our purposes, is that it is used as evidence that the soul is capable of living apart from the body. Apparently, we could even go to the "third heaven" in this disembodied state.

Let's start with what is most apparent; Paul seems to be referring to the third heaven and paradise in exactly the same way within this section. That is, the word "paradise" is used to give rhetorical force and emphasis to the "third heaven" that is mentioned in the previous verse. For all intents and purposes, they appear to be synonymous. The "third heaven" may have been a reference

---

[52] Paul Achtemeier, Joel Green, and Marianne Meye, *Introducing the New Testament*, 352.

to something like the furthest part of the heavens, where God Himself was thought to dwell.[53] Whatever it means, it is certainly a very sacred place that is beyond the scope of normal human comprehension (v. 4). It's also not merely just heaven, being that Paul designates it as more than that; this is the "third heaven." We can wonder—is this the same place that Jesus referred to during his encounter with the criminal on the cross? It's possible, but highly unlikely. Among other things, we would need to speculate as to why a deathbed conversion of sorts would bring one to such a heavenly dwelling place when even the greatest believers of the past (Elijah and Enoch notwithstanding) simply went to Sheol (the grave). It makes better sense that Jesus intended paradise to be thought of as the heavenly Kingdom that the criminal would someday enjoy. I will assess that particular passage in more detail in the next section. For the moment, we still need to address another issue within this passage in 2 Corinthians: what Paul's use of the phrase "in the body or out of the body" means in this particular context.

As opposed to Philippians 1:22-24, where Paul used the term *sarx* (flesh), the word used to express this otherworldly adventure is *soma* (body). As we previously saw, this is the same word used repeatedly in 1 Corinthians 15, where Paul discussed the necessity of bodily existence.[54] On two separate occasions, Paul mentioned that he was not sure whether or not his heavenly journey occurred while he was within his own body (*soma*). The first important thing to notice is that Paul did not say "in the body or *as a soul/spirit*." As far as the actual terminology is concerned, he was not openly inviting the reader to think of this as a "physical body *vs.* immaterial spirit" issue. Remember, Paul made it clear to the same group of people (the Corinthians) that such a thing is nonsense (1 Cor. 15).

This means that Paul was not attempting to say that he had left his body as a conscious spirit, for the purpose of venturing off to the heavenly realm. But if this is true, what did Paul mean when he said this *may* have occurred "out of the body?" While he did not use the expression "in the spirit," there is a sense in which he must have meant something sort of like this. If he was not physically there, then he must have been present in some way that we might

---

[53] See Kent Philpott's article, *"The Third Heaven:" The Apostle Paul and Kat Kerr.*
[54] See the section "I'll Fly Away" in chapter 1, for the explanation of the term "body."

think of as "spiritual." The author of Revelation[55] had a similar experience when he was shown all of the fantastic things he later recorded in the text (see 1:10 and 4:2, for example). To both Paul and John, the heavenly journey was certainly unimaginable for those of us who aren't privy to such experiences.

The key to these examples from Scripture is that nothing really suggests that the events were anything different than visions of heaven and a variety of events. The expressions "in the Spirit," as John used, and "out of the body," as Paul used, do not directly lend themselves to the idea that a soul is capable of consciously leaving the body and later returning. And here we are again. If the two options are that Paul either had heavenly visions or a full-blown trip (as a disembodied spirit) to a distant part of the heavens, we must ask which one makes the best sense of things as a whole. Despite the biblical evidence against it, many people still opt to believe that Paul travelled to another destination as a disembodied spirit.

This may be an appropriate place to briefly pause and discuss the issue of near-death experiences (or NDEs) because they are often used as evidence that the soul could consciously venture elsewhere apart from the body (which is exactly how some view Paul's experience). Take the case of Howard Storm, for example. Storm, a former atheist professor turned Christian, received a lot of notoriety for his account of traveling to hell during an alleged NDE. In his book, *My Descent into Death*, Storm describes a horrific place of torment where some type of entities attacked and mutilated him. This is particularly interesting when we consider that neither Satan nor the demons currently exist in such a place.[56] Another well-known example of a near-death experience is Colton Burpo's account of seeing his deceased grandfather—whom he would later identify in a family photograph—during an emergency surgery.[57] It's worth noting that a very similar story, which is documented in the book, *The Boy Who Went to Heaven*, was officially denounced as a hoax in January of 2015.[58]

---

[55] Though church tradition holds that the apostle John is the author of Revelation, scholars have questioned this notion for centuries. One of the predominant problems is that the book is typically dated to the mid 90's AD, which would make John an extremely old man at that time. Still, he may have indeed been the author and there certainly isn't enough evidence to discount this view.

[56] I discuss this point further in the section entitled, "Satan's Domain," at the beginning of chapter four.

[57] This event is described within the book, *Heaven is for Real*.

[58] Tara Fowler, "Little Boy Who 'Came Back from Heaven' Says He Made It Up."

Furthermore, NDERF (the Near Death Experience Research Foundation) has documented thousands of NDEs from across the globe. A short sampling of these otherworldly experiences yields no shortage of variation. In one account, we read about a woman who turned into a "golden orb," and later proceeded to converse (in Orbese, I suppose) with other orbs before returning to her body.[59] Another account described a man who flew around his city with an unknown companion before coming back to his body.[60] Yet another story described a woman's heavenly "playtime," in which she jumped around on the clouds like a child before coming back to earth.[61] Thousands of others could be mentioned, but the point should be clear enough.

While there seems to be at least a degree of continuity within *some* NDEs (like visions of tunnels, lights, deceased relatives, etc.), the problem is that such accounts are far too disparate to be taken as concrete evidence in favor of the TDP. One person reports having gone to heaven, another to hell, another to infinite darkness, another to a place resembling a hospital waiting room, and so on. Within these different locations, the type of existence recounted by the revived individual also drastically varies. Some claimed to have a body, others only a soul, and still others report all sorts of things in between (recall the glowing orbs).

Furthermore, some report to have seen Mohammed, while others saw Jesus, while still others saw the gods or goddesses of pagan religions, and all manner of other prophets and deities. While it would be rash to dismiss every person who claims to have had such an experience, it is also clear that not all of these realities can be valid at once. This is especially true when we consider that the only two biblical possibilities for disembodied existence would be in either heaven or hell, or the separated planes of another intermediate place (like Abraham's bosom and Sheol/Hades). Certainly, not all forms of NDEs can be used to suggest these possibilities. These accounts cannot provide evidence for the TDP because of the enormous discrepancies in detail. As I will later discuss in more depth,[62] differing accounts of an event or an experience prove very little beyond the fact that no one is sure what is actually true.

---

[59] Nderf.org, NDE 3670

[60] Ibid. NDE 3149.

[61] Ibid. NDE 3295.

[62] See the section entitled "A Foot in Every Door," at the end of chapter three, for a more detailed description of this point.

For example, if the gospels radically varied in their descriptions of the risen Christ (which they do not), it would be very difficult to defend his resurrection as an objective event. The skeptics would have a field day, and rightfully so. Furthermore, we simply must remember that NDEs are not the tales of those who have truly gone on to the afterlife. Rather, they are mysterious events described by people who were temporarily unconscious or were even pronounced dead for a *very* brief period of time. It is perhaps conceivable that we may be able to experience something in the small amount of time when our souls discorporate from our bodies: when the "information" leaves the body, in my view. Even if true, this would also fail to tell us about what happens to those who completely die (i.e. are not resuscitated). More likely though, and as I suggest concerning both Paul's and John's experiences, NDEs (if generally valid) make much better sense as *visions* of places or ideas beyond normal comprehension than as journeys undertaken by disembodied souls.

To get back to Paul's understanding of things, it has been a central point within this book that he was not fond of the idea that we could be living beings without physical bodies; it is clear from the beginning that it doesn't work this way (Gen. 2:7). This means that when Paul said he could have been "in the body or out of the body," it does not mean he was either there physically or there in spirit form. Instead, it means that he wasn't sure if the whole trip had been a literal occurrence or a vision. It was apparently so vivid that Paul could not tell if he had actually gone to the "third heaven," or had only been given a miraculous glimpse of it. The latter would make better sense of Paul's experience and his insistence that we are not simply souls temporarily living within bodies. But there is still one more element of the passage that is worth considering.

For the sake of discussion, let's say that Paul traveled to the "third heaven" as a disembodied spirit. What would this really do to aid the cause of those who believe we depart to heaven, or another conscious interim realm, upon death? In this scenario, Paul was alive, and then was literally taken to the "third heaven" as a spirit. Meanwhile, his physical body remained on earth somewhere until he returned to it (it's worth wondering where his body stayed during this time). Even if all of this were true, it says nothing about what happens when *we die*. Paul was clearly not dead, after all. Again, we must remember a very important element of this passage: Paul wasn't even sure how he had experienced the event. It could even be possible that this was just something that Paul was able to enjoy as the apostle to the Gentiles: a special privilege, if you will, that doesn't say a thing about the rest of us. Clearly, few people are given such an opportunity. Whatever the case, it hardly serves as solid evidence that we go to some immaterial state of conscious existence when we die. Basing a theological doctrine on an event that was clearly hazy to Paul himself is simply not exegetically forthright. That being said, we must press on towards other texts that speak about the state of the dead.

PROWLERS IN PARADISE

While it would be difficult to say that any passage of Scripture has been referenced more often than those previously discussed, Jesus' dialogue with the criminal on the cross has garnered its fair share of attention over the years. This text is also considered to be strong evidence for the TDP and the overall notion that the soul continues in conscious existence after death. In this account, Jesus is hanging on his cross beside two men who actually admit that they are guilty of crimes against the Roman Empire (Lk. 23:41). While those on the ground level are doing their best to verbally abuse Jesus in his time of suffering, a surprising theological discussion is taking place several feet above the crowd:

> "One of the criminals who hung there hurled insults at him: 'Aren't you the Messiah? Save yourself and us!' But the other criminal rebuked him. 'Don't you fear God,' he said, 'since you are under the same sentence? We are punished justly, for we are getting what our deeds deserve. But this man has done nothing wrong.' Then he said, 'Jesus, remember me when you come into your kingdom.' Jesus answered him, 'Truly I tell you, today you will be with me in paradise.'"[63]

Perhaps the most shocking thing about this passage is that we find Jesus concerning himself with the salvation of a criminal, even when he is personally just a few hours away from death. Unfortunately, that point is frequently glossed over in favor of using this passage as a proof-text for certain theological perspectives. While it is occasionally used to prove that baptism is not necessary for salvation (the criminal was saved without being baptized), it is also frequently considered to speak to the issue of the afterlife.

---

[63] Luke 23:39-43.

The argument is fairly straightforward: the man put his faith in Jesus as they hung on their crosses together, and Jesus honored his declaration by telling him they would "be in paradise" together. Simple enough, right? From that point on, it gets considerably more complicated. The passage is nearly always translated with the comma after the word "you" and before the word "today," as it is shown above in the NIV. The problem is that while most interpreters agree with this translation, all acknowledge the fact that the comma could potentially go elsewhere:[64] say, *after* the word "today." In fact, there was not initially a comma present in the entire verse at all. One needs only to compare several modern versions of a given passage to see that the placement of punctuation marks can vary noticeably after the translation process.

The language in which the New Testament was predominantly written is known as Koine Greek, which is different from our English language in many ways. This is not the place for an entire lesson on this language, and there are other scholars who would be better equipped to provide one. For our purposes, it is worth mentioning that the original Greek manuscripts (called "autographs") of the New Testament most likely did not include a feature that is equivalent to our modern comma. It was largely up to the skilled readers of the community, who were expected to be proficient in the Greek language, to arrive at such breaks and pauses by evaluating the overall context of the words. The original texts were primarily meant to be read aloud to gathered communities, because there simply weren't many copies to go around. Later generations of scribes would need to apply much of the punctuation as they copied the texts and translated the earliest manuscripts into various languages. This ultimately means that those whom we have entrusted to translate our contemporary versions of the Bible have to decide where to place the commas. For the most part, they are placed at very logical positions, as we can see when we read them today. It also means, however, that comma placement (and, at times, other punctuation marks) is up for debate. This passage is a very good example of where that debate can (and has) taken place.

If we are holding to the normal translation of the passage, where the comma is placed before "today," then this particular text can actually read very differently than it otherwise might. *Most phrases do not*, but this one certainly does. This is what I mean: with the comma existing before "today,"

---

[64] Leon Morris, *The Tyndale New Testament Commentaries: Luke*, 359.

we would interpret Jesus' statement as a pronouncement that both he and the criminal would be entering "paradise" immediately upon their deaths (the very day they passed away). But if we slide that comma back *just one word*, placing it after "today," the text reads much differently. For simplicity's sake, let's examine the two translations together.

> Truly I tell you, *today* you will be with me in paradise.

> Truly I tell you *today*, you will be with me in paradise.

See the difference? If the second rendering is correct, then Jesus would simply be telling the man (on that day) that he would *someday* be with him in paradise. Thus, the difference is both simple and profound.

Based on the placement of the comma as being either before or after the word "today," we have the difference between existing in paradise that very day or at some undisclosed point in the future. Being that the comma actually could be placed at either spot, we are forced to ask which position would make the most sense with regards to the overall discussion of when/where we go after death. None of this information is new to biblical scholars, or even many lay people, but it still remains a valid point that must be factored into any interpretation of this particular passage. While you can assess the biblical evidence concerning the state of the dead in the entirety of this book, it would be most helpful at the moment to think about this question logically. The debate should revolve around this question: where did *Jesus* go when he died that day on the cross? If Jesus' statement was that the criminal would be with him in paradise, then when the criminal went to paradise would be inextricably bound to when Jesus did. When the issue is considered in this way, it may actually be easier to answer.

The Son of God became incarnate in the man Jesus for many reasons. He came to preach, to instruct, to more fully reveal God's character to the world, to replace Adam as the Head of Humanity, and he most certainly came to atone for the sins of the world. In doing so, Jesus began the process of mending the broken relationship between us and God that has existed since Adam and Eve's rebellion. But the final, and perhaps most crucial, element of Jesus' ministry is that he conquered death. As Paul so crucially noted, if Jesus was not actually raised from the dead then our faith has been in vain; our sins would still remain, and any hope for the afterlife would be destroyed (1 Cor.15:14-18). A savior who does not eliminate our ultimate problem (death) is no *savior* at all. But how did Jesus actually conquer death? The obvious response is that he accomplished this by rising from the dead (i.e. through resurrection). In order to do such a thing, however, Jesus must truly have been dead in the first place: deceased, gone, completely and utterly vanquished from the realm of the living. Remember, death is the absence of life. If it were not so, then we would simply refer to the "transitions of life," or something equivalent.

Some modern thinkers are making this very connection. In an article about the resurrection in the *Princeton Theological Review*, theologian Adam Kotsko astutely observes the problem:

> "Yet how is the notion of a soul that can never die compatible with the crossing of the boundaries between life and death that we see in resurrection? Resurrection is certainly an overcoming of death, but it is far from an exclusion of it after all, Jesus still carries the marks of his death on his resurrected body. And what sense can Jesus' and, by extension, our solidarity with the dead make if the dead are not really dead?"[65]

The key is in the last phrase, concerning the logical necessity that the "dead" are actually just that—dead. In the present context, the point is fairly straightforward: *In order to conquer death for humanity, Jesus needed to die (really die) as the rest of humanity does.* This means that when Jesus' body rested in the tomb, like other bodies do, it could be said that he had departed to the realm of the dead (Sheol). Again, this simply means that he was actually dead in the grave, not that he consciously went to the underground labyrinth for souls that many Greeks envisioned in their particular views of Hades. If he had not actually gone to the grave, then Jesus would not have been fully human.

The way in which we should interpret Jesus' use of the term "spirit," however, is quite another story. Mainly, this term is difficult (if not impossible) to fully comprehend here because the Son of God is an eternal, preexistent being rather than a created being. In other words, he did not have the breath of life placed into him (i.e. he did not begin to exist) as Adam did. If things had operated this way, then he would have ceased to be divine. Indeed, this is the paradox of the God-man; the Son began to exist as a human being

---

[65] Adam Kotsko, "The Resurrection of the Dead: A Religionless Interpretation."

in the man Jesus, but he did not begin to exist *as God* at that time. But what did it mean for Jesus to give his spirit back to the Father at his death? Was this an indication that he expected to live as a disembodied being in heaven immediately after his crucifixion?

While many have taken this passage to mean just that, it should not be taken in such a way. It is crucial to note that, in this particular passage, we are not dealing with the word "soul." Instead, we are dealing with the word "spirit." This is where things begin to get very interesting. We read that Jesus gave his spirit back to the Father at his death (23:46), and a couple of points need to be mentioned here. While the word *pneuma* (spirit) is being used here rather than *psuche* (soul), it should not be viewed as some completely different incorporeal human component. The term "spirit" is mentioned in a vast number of ways throughout the Bible.[66] When it refers to the driving force of the human body, as it certainly does in this particular passage, it should not be equated with our normal conceptions of the human soul. As it is used here, the spirit is what causes us to simply be alive, and is certainly not the information that contains our personal identities and the connection between mortal existence and glorified existence: what we call the "soul." Further, to view the spirit as an entirely different immaterial element would be to imply that a human being is comprised of his or her own body, soul, *and* spirit, as though they were literally three different components.

While it's quite true that Platonism and certain other Greek philosophies often regarded the spirit as being the immaterial vehicle for the soul—and the basis of the soul's union with the body[67]—this was not so much the case in biblical thought. This type of "trilism" would probably have caused most believers' heads to spin. The apostle Paul, for example, was certainly aware of the various brands of Greek philosophy, particularly the many aspects of Stoic thought. Still, Paul ended up proposing a relationship between the soul and the spirit that is in direct contrast to the Platonic views of the day. To Paul, the soul was inferior to the spirit.[68] This would make sense because Paul consistently used the term *pneuma* in association with the Spirit of God rather than as some additional incorporeal component of a human being.[69] He associated the term with life and the giver of life (the Spirit). I would

---

[66] Refer to Carl Schultz's, "Spirit," for a look at the various meanings of this word.

[67] Christopher A. Plaisance, "The Transvaluation of 'Soul' and 'Spirit'," 256.

[68] Ibid. 260-264.

[69] Ibid. 262.

suggest that this was a common early Christian understanding of the "spirit," and this is precisely what all human beings give back to God at death. The Spirit of God, as the giver and sustainer of life, receives back the life each one of us is blessed to have been given. God gave life to Adam and all who would come after him. When we die, we give that life back to our Creator. This is essentially what Jesus intended with his declaration, "Father, into your hands I commit my spirit" (Lk. 23:46).

It is clear that Jesus did give his spirit back to the Father, but this was essentially his way of saying that he was accepting his death and was aware that he was breathing his last breaths. Put another way, this was Jesus' method of expressing that he was willingly returning to God what God had graciously given—the gift of life. This passage is not about Jesus' "inner being" consciously going to heaven during the time between his death and resurrection. It is not about his soul shedding the mortal body in order to live by itself in splendor for parts of three days following the Crucifixion. It is not about any of this. This passage is about one thing: Jesus dying an agonizing, human death, and the promise that death would not be the end. It would not be the end for him, and it would not ultimately be the end for the criminal at his side, either.

As complex as this whole discussion can be, the crux of the point is that Jesus could not have gone somewhere that the rest of humanity does not go upon death. That is, unless, we want to say that he didn't actually experience death as we do. As I mentioned earlier, this would defeat the entire purpose of conquering death as a human being. Since we go to the grave, Jesus must also have done so. In fairness, I will admit that my interpretation of this passage is not without its difficulties. We do not know for certain how the dynamics of being the incarnate Son of God and dying a mortal death played out in every way. What I have offered is an honest attempt to grapple with all of these complexities and postulate something that is concrete enough to understand. But these conclusions seem to be within reason based on the previous arguments, as well as the way that the Bible (as a whole) portrays concepts like Sheol and the body-soul relationship.

After this assessment, you may be wondering what all of this has to do with the passage we were originally looking at. In short, it has everything to do with it. If I am correct (or close to it) concerning Jesus' experience in death, then we would have a perspective that differs from the status quo. Jesus told the criminal that he would be with him in *paradeisos*, which we translate as "paradise."[70] Shockingly, this term appears only three times in the entire New Testament (one of which was previously covered in 2 Cor. 12:2-4), with just one of those references (here in v. 43) belonging to Jesus. The final use of this term is found in Revelation 2:7, which is discussed momentarily.

In Jewish thought, as well as the early Christian perspective, paradise could actually refer to several different things. In some rabbinic traditions, paradise was thought of as the place of bliss that man had lost after the Fall. As time went on, it later came to be referred to by some as the place occupied by fallen saints. Some have speculated that Jesus' use of the phrase "Abraham's bosom," as seen in the parable of the Rich Man and Lazarus, is synonymous with "paradise," and that it displays Jesus' agreement that deceased believers go on to live there during the interim period.[71] Of course, why not simply say "paradise" if that was the intended meaning? It is difficult to say precisely what Jesus meant in using this term; he personally used it nowhere else, so we have little context for Jesus' perspective about it. The reality that the word had several connotations within the New Testament, along with the point about the placement of the comma near the word "today," should at least indicate that it would be difficult to couch any firm perspective about the state of dead on this passage. It should be considered as a piece of the puzzle, at best. Realistically, there are far too many variables at play here to use this passage as evidence of what happens when *we* die.

Given the fact that Jesus' supposed trip to a conscious existence after the Crucifixion would not be consistent with what we know about the realm of the dead, we cannot conclude that the criminal next to him went to such a place at his death, either. It's simply more reasonable to believe that Jesus meant this in the *ultimate* sense (as Paul did). This means that paradise would most likely refer to the new heavens and the new earth (the finished Kingdom) rather than to some intermediate place of the dead. It would also mean that the comma would make better sense if it were to follow the word "today" rather than precede it. For that matter, does the comma need to show up in either spot? In theory, the word "today" may even appear elsewhere; "Truly, *today* I tell you, you will be with me in paradise." You get the idea. If the comma is placed *anywhere* other than before the word "today," the incredible complexity of Jesus' peculiar position as both God and man is

---

[70] Luke 23:43.

[71] H.A. Kent Jr., "Paradise," 891.

completely resolved. We need not speculate on where the disembodied Jesus ventured, or what he did during that time.

If this passage is viewed as describing Jesus' (and the criminal's) *ultimate* existence in the new heavens and new earth, then we are simply dealing with the risen Jesus who has returned to his rightful place at the right hand of the Father; Jesus' mortal condition no longer exists. Finally, the fact that Jesus used the term *pneuma* (spirit) rather than *psuche* (soul) definitively tells us that this statement was not about his conscious soul returning to heaven that day, but about the sustaining power of the Spirit departing. Jesus' soul did not travel to a conscious realm of the dead while his body remained in the tomb, and neither did the criminal's. It is very important to keep in mind that none of the gospels ever mention Jesus during the time between the Crucifixion and the Resurrection. He was never seen as a disembodied spirit, nor even discussed in such a way. He was embodied when he died, and embodied when he rose. Anything else is more or less just speculation.

One other quick point must be made here. If my interpretation is completely incorrect, and this passage really is suggesting that Jesus' soul consciously departed to heaven that very day, it would actually still work to prove one of my other points in this book. It would close the door on the belief that Jesus went to free the saints of the past—those individuals being disembodied, of course—immediately after he died.[72] How could Jesus return to the Father in heaven *and* go to a conscious realm of the dead at the same time? If one tries to make the case that Jesus' divinity would allow him to be present in both places at once, they should remember that the thief must also have been able to do so. Try as they might, interpreters cannot have it both ways.

At the end of the day, it is simply more logical to believe that this passage was about Jesus giving his life back to the Father, and the reality that the criminal's request would be granted; the man would indeed be with Jesus when he "came into his kingdom." While this does not make perfect sense of all the factors involved, there are far fewer loose ends and highly debatable positions to deal with in this interpretation. This, of course, is the goal. We should seek the view that best unifies Scripture and resolves logical conflicts. With all of this being said, we are prepared to finish the discussion about Jesus' words to the criminal. To paraphrase Jesus' intention in the statement, we could interpret the situation as follows: Jesus was telling the man *that*

---

[72] See the section entitled "Descending into Hell," in chapter three.

day that he would *ultimately* be with him, when he returned *in the fullness of the Kingdom.* This understanding of the word "paradise" would be consistent with John's use in Revelation 2:7, which is specifically about the ultimate place of blessedness: the new heavens and new earth.[73]

Just one more thing should be added. Even if every one of these points were abandoned—granting that both Jesus and the criminal went directly to heaven as spirits on the day they were crucified—the reality is that it wouldn't necessarily say anything about what will happen to each of us when *we* die. This event would give us the exception, not the rule. Like the slew of examples I discuss in chapter three,[74] the criminal's experience does not directly describe what will happen to each of us any more than Elijah's ascension does. This was a unique situation that speaks to the fate of the criminal and no one else. To stretch the meaning further is to simply speculate.

In order to provide an explanation about what is true for *all* believers, we must look at passages that are literally intended to speak about all believers. In other words, we need to find teachings that are intended to discuss the universal state of humanity rather than isolated circumstances that only pertain to certain people. Beyond Paul's teachings in 1 Corinthians 15 and 1 Thessalonians 4:13-18, most of the passages evaluated thus far do not fit this criterion. In chapter four, I will add more passages of clarification to this list. But for now, we move to the next biblical possibility concerning the interim period—the realm of the dead. While these passages will reveal stories that venture well into the world of the strange and the bizarre—or even the macabre—we may actually find that they further darken what is an already muddled pond. As I said at the onset of this book, the state of the dead is hardly a black-and-white issue.

---

[73] George R. Beasley-Murray, *New Bible Commentary*, 1428.

[74] See the section entitled, "The Return of Samuel," for examples of events that are biblical exceptions to the normal rules of operation.

CHAPTER THREE

SOMEWHERE *UNDER* THE RAINBOW

T hough it may sound foreign to many people, heaven and hell are not the only two possible interim destinations that the Bible can be interpreted as suggesting. While we all may end up at one of those two places, there are some who believe that we make a stop somewhere well before that. The Catholic doctrine of Purgatory suggests that some believers will need to be refined in a purifying realm prior to their final existence in Christ's Kingdom. I will deal with this view separately in chapter five because I consider it to have special theological significance, but I'll note here that I find the biblical evidence for Purgatory to be almost entirely lacking. It is frequently missed, however, that many Protestants also believe that we will enter into a disembodied, transitional realm of existence during the period between death and the resurrection. There is a "second option" within the TDP (the *temporary-disembodiment position*), if you will.

This realm of existence is also for those who have died, but await a body that is fit to inhabit the new heavens and new earth (again, that is the ultimate goal of the Christian faith). We can almost think of this as a third possible realm of existence. There is the world we live in, God's heavenly realm (which will someday fully merge with our world), and then the temporary realm for those who live between the two. While most people do not distinguish between these realms and those of heaven and hell, a distinction simply must be made. As I will illustrate, the following passages *cannot* be describing a conscious intermediate existence in heaven or hell. By extension, we simply cannot lump all of the passages that can be used as evidence for a conscious, intermediate state into one neat package. While the final section of the chapter specifically discusses this point in detail, I want you (the reader) to pay close attention to how the realm of the dead differs from both heaven and hell.

The Bible, as some see it, could be alluding to the realm of the dead in passages that speak to the so-called "Harrowing of Hell." These mainly include Ephesians 4:7-10, and 1 Peter 3:18-20 and 4:6. Other passages and stories that may speak to this realm include Matthew 27:52, the parable of the Rich Man and Lazarus (Lk. 16:19-31), and even the story of Samuel's appearance from the dead (1 Sam. 28). Throughout the course of this chapter, I will evaluate all of these passages both as they pertain to the interim period and how they constitute an often hidden, second view within the TDP. We will discover that the passages of Scripture that are used to support this belief range from the theologically ambiguous to the downright bizarre.

The Rich and the Dead

The story of the Rich Man and Lazarus is one of the go-to examples from Scripture for those who believe that our souls consciously survive death during the interim period. Though only the Gospel of Luke contains this story (16:19-31), it is one of Jesus' better known parables, as it tells of a situation that is all-too-common within every generation of people—the "haves" and the "have-nots." Essentially, the story goes as follows: there is an unnamed wealthy man who encounters a poor beggar named Lazarus on his way to and from his estate, on what is apparently a regular basis. The rich man "lives in luxury every day," while Lazarus is financially destitute and is living on the streets outside the rich man's property. To make matters worse, Lazarus is most likely a leper (v. 20), and is regarded by others as being even lower than the dogs that came to lick his wounds. Though not directly stated, it is clearly inferred that the rich man cared nothing for Lazarus and was quite content to maintain their radically different living conditions. Thus, the story tells of a cruel-minded person of means and a kind-hearted person of poverty. For this reason, it is strongly implied that Lazarus was religiously faithful and the rich man was spiritually bankrupt.

As the story progresses, we learn that the two men end up in even more drastically different situations after they pass away; Lazarus is taken to "Abraham's bosom," while the rich man is given a desolate spot in "hell" (v. 23). While in torment, the rich man sees Abraham and Lazarus living in comfort and proceeds to *beg* for relief from his condition. Abraham responds by telling the man that he cannot help him because of the impassable "chasm" that exists between their two resting places (v. 26). The more specific reason is that he was now receiving the judgment he had stored up during his earthly life; the rich man had his "good things" and, handling them so irreverently, was now relegated to an afterlife of pain and torment. In some sense, we could compare the rich man's fate to that of Ebenezer Scrooge, prior to Scrooge's miraculous turnabout.

As the story reaches its climactic end, the rich man again *begs* Abraham to send Lazarus (of all people) back to warn his family, so that they may turn from their paths and be spared his fate (v. 27). Once again, Abraham is forced to decline the man's request on the basis that his family would not heed that warning, either. As a clear reference to what Jesus would later do, Abraham further explains that the rich man's family would not believe, ". . . even if someone rises from the dead" (v. 31)! Before moving on, please note that the rich man is asking Abraham for help rather than God. This alone suggests that the realms we are dealing with here are not heaven and hell because, if they were, the rich man would presumably be asking God to intercede instead.

There is a whole lot going on in this story, to be sure. To view this passage as one whose meaning is intended to discuss the nature of the afterlife is to begin in the wrong place, but we'll get to that. The main point of this story actually has to do with the Judeo-Christian concept of retribution theology. Retribution theology is essentially a term having to do with the ways in which God is believed to administer justice within our world: how God is thought to give everyone their just *retribution*, if you will. Early in Jewish history, "retributive justice" was the dominant explanation for this issue, and it ultimately asserts that God deals out the proper reward or punishment within one's lifetime. This can be clearly seen in the general proverbial maxim, "Whoever digs a pit will fall into it; if someone rolls a stone, it will roll back on them" (26:27).

Over time, the general principles of retributive justice became dogmatic recipes for how God intervenes within our world. When the exile proved that God may not administer justice quite so mechanically—Assyria and Babylon were getting away with their wickedness—the Jewish beliefs about retribution theology began to shift. The perspective of "ultimate retribution" (as I would call it) began to emerge, and would go on to dominate the theology of the New Testament. In short, this means that there is—whether in this world or the next—a reversal of fortunes that will take place in people's lives.[75] If you lived a godless life, you would be condemned in the next life. If you lived a faithful and obedient life, then you would be rewarded in the next life. In other words, God deals out justice more in the eschatological (or final) sense than in the present sense. This is completely consistent with a message like that of Jesus' parable of the Weeds, which I discuss later.

While there is an entire history of development and a great deal of detail that could be discussed regarding the issue of retribution theology, this understanding will suffice for our purposes. With this information in mind, the central point of the parable of the Rich Man and Lazarus becomes more apparent. The life you choose to live in this world has clear and irrevocable consequences in the next, whether positive or negative. In this sense, Jesus intended the story to be a powerful warning to everyone who would hear it. We are all paving our eternal destinies, brick by brick, right now. *This life* is where we make the choices that will determine everything that happens in the hereafter. Another crucial point is made in the final dialogue between the rich man and Abraham. While we may ask God for more and more evidence to believe, the reality is that no amount of proof will ever appease those who constantly require that God show Himself. Jesus was raised from the dead, yet the majority of people who should have believed this still failed to do so (even the apostles, at first). Though others could be mentioned, these two points are truly the essential teachings of the story.

I previously stated that looking into this parable for literal information about the afterlife is to begin in the wrong place altogether, and I will now clarify what I meant by that. The first point that should be mentioned is that we can immediately dismiss any concepts of heaven and hell from the discussion. For starters, no serious interpreter should attempt to equate "Abraham's bosom" with the heavenly realm presently occupied by God and the angels. In his sermon on the parable of the Rich Man and Lazarus, John Wesley pointed out that Abraham's bosom—which he equates with "paradise"—is not heaven:

> "'The beggar died:' Here ended poverty and pain: -- 'And
> was carried by angels;' nobler servants than any that attended

---

[75] Though much of Bart Ehrman's scholarship is questionable in terms of its purposes, he does provide a good discussion of the "reversal of fortunes" involved in retribution theology. See *God's Problem*, 222-225.

the rich man; -- 'into Abraham's bosom:' -- So the Jews commonly termed what our blessed Lord styles paradise; the place 'where the wicked cease from troubling, and where the weary are at rest;' the receptacle of holy souls, from death to the resurrection. It is, indeed, very generally supposed, that the souls of good men, as soon as they are discharged from the body, go directly to heaven; but this opinion has not the least foundation in the oracles of God: On the contrary, our Lord says to Mary, after the resurrection, 'Touch me not; for I am not yet ascended to my Father' in heaven. But he had been in paradise, according to his promise to the penitent thief: 'This day shalt thou be with me in paradise.' Hence, it is plain, that paradise is not heaven. It is indeed (if we may be allowed the expression) the antechamber of heaven, where the souls of the righteous remain till, after the general judgment, they are received into glory."[76]

While Wesley's view that Abraham's bosom is synonymous with "paradise" is questionable,[77] his point that the positive realm discussed in this parable should not be linked with heaven is completely on target. One could say that Abraham's bosom is a title for an intermediate existence (between this life/body and the next) and that it is somehow *like* heaven (as Wesley suggested), but the case cannot be made that Abraham's bosom *is* heaven itself.

As I mentioned earlier, others have speculated that Abraham's bosom is a reference to the Jewish concept of paradise.[78] If we remember, Jesus used this term in his dealings with the criminal on the cross. While that particular term is better left as a reference to the ultimate place of bliss that believers will experience when the Kingdom has come in its fullness, Abraham's bosom cannot be taken in the same way. On the other side, the parable is not talking about "hell" as we understand it, either. This is certainly a place of discomfort according to the passage itself (v. 23), but it's not *the* place of torment that will house the destruction of Satan, the demons, and the unrepentant at the end of the age (Rev. 20:10-15).

The word Jesus used in this passage is Hades, which is historically

---

[76] John Wesley, "The Sermons of John Wesley - Sermon 112."

[77] I discussed the term "paradise" in much greater detail in the section entitled, "Prowlers in Paradise," in chapter two.

[78] K.S. Kantzer, "Paradise." *Evangelical Dictionary of Biblical Theology*, 891.

understood as a hazy, negative existence in death. In the New Testament, it normally functions in similar fashion to the Hebrew Sheol, which essentially refers only to the place where the dead go (i.e. the grave). In the sense that death is the end of life and the event which serves as one of the most agonizing penalties of the Fall, it clearly had negative connotations. Hades is not, however, the fiery pits of everlasting destruction that the New Testament often refers to. If Jesus was speaking about the "lake of fire," the place of ultimate destruction, or the place where there will be "weeping and gnashing of teeth," then he would have used the word Gehenna. *Gehenna* is the term Jesus used to describe the final place of punishment for Satan and his followers, not Hades. The distinguished theologian Robert P. Lightner correctly observed this point, saying, "Whereas Hades is the intermediate state, Gehenna is eternal hell. Wherever it is used in the NT, it always means the place of eternal damnation."[79]

While the second letter of Peter refers to "Tartarus"[80]—which was, to many Greeks of that day, the lowest level found within all of Hades—it is also not directly equivalent to the lake of fire, either. Gehenna, not Tartarus or Hades, is the everlasting abode of the wicked in biblical thought. It is very telling (and biblically consistent) that Jesus used the word Hades here rather than Gehenna. On the other end of the spectrum, if Jesus intended us to think of heaven, then why didn't he just say so? Furthermore, why did he speak of Lazarus as going to father Abraham for comfort rather than to Father God? Clearly, this is not heaven—the dwelling place of God and the angels—that we are talking about here. For these reasons, we can dismiss the concepts of heaven and hell from a proper interpretation of this parable. In truth, this point actually poses another major problem for the TDP. One cannot combine this story with passages that allegedly speak about going to heaven, or attempt to use both as common evidence of a disembodied interim period. I discuss this in greater detail at the end of the chapter. For now, we must return to the story.

If the tale is not discussing heaven and hell, then is it talking about a place of disembodied existence between this life and those destinations? If you are casually working your way through this passage, then the answer could *appear* to be yes. Certainly, Jesus' message was about two people who died and went to very different realms of existence. Could the parable be referring

---

[79] R.P. Lightner, *Evangelical Dictionary of Biblical Theology*, 548.
[80] 2 Peter 2:4.

to some type of temporary holding place for the souls of the dead? There are very good reasons to reject this idea. As most of us know, Jesus' favorite teaching tool was the parable. By any proper definition, a parable is a fictional story that is intended to illustrate a greater spiritual truth about God and His Kingdom. This means that the events themselves did not actually occur, but the truths they represent are very real. If we turn several pages back from the parable of the Rich Man and Lazarus, we find other parables surrounding it. One of the tell-tale signs of a parable is the following introduction: "there was a _____ person" (man/woman/master/etc.), with the blank typically being the main variable within the opening to a parable. You could also insert the words "rich" or "young" into the blank, for example.

Traveling just one story back in the Gospel of Luke, we find the parable of the Shrewd Manager. Not surprisingly, the story begins with the words "there was a *rich man*." Sound familiar? If we go one more story back, we see the parable of the Prodigal Son. As you might imagine, it also begins with the words "there was a *man*." While the two stories that precede the Lost Son do not display the typical introduction pattern, they are also clearly parables being that they begin with figurative "suppose X happened" scenarios. Just like the two parables that precede it, the Rich Man and Lazarus opens with storybook, "there was a (rich) man," introduction.

The point I am making here is very simple. No one is claiming that there was really a son who asked for his inheritance and ended up living with pigs, or that there was really a business manager who decreased the obligation of his master's debtors, or that there was really a person who owned one hundred sheep and went off looking for the one that wandered away, or any of the like. All of these scenarios are plausible, but whether or not these stories were based on real situations was clearly not the point. In his day, John Wycliffe correctly noted that this parable should not be used to prove our condition after death (i.e. be taken literally),[81] and N.T. Wright—one of the world's most distinguished contemporary biblical scholars—has said the same.[82] On that note, so would every legitimate biblical scholar on the planet; that is, if we were talking about any parable besides this one.

Whether we are looking at the way they are constructed, or the lessons they are intended to teach, it is relatively easy to spot a parable. Even the famous book of Job reveals signs that it may be a story or parable (albeit,

---

[81] "Immortality of the Soul in the Bible?"
[82] N.T. Wright, *Surprised by Hope*, 176-77.

a very large one) about the nation of Israel.[83] So the question is this: why shouldn't we treat the story of the Rich Man and Lazarus like any other parable? Anyone who views the story as a literal explanation of the interim period is forced to assert that it should be treated differently because the poor man is given a name (Lazarus). John Calvin summarized this position when he battled the proponents of soul sleep back in the sixteenth century, saying:

> "To secure a means of escape, they make the history a parable, and say, that all which truth speaks concerning Abraham, the rich man and the poor man, is fiction. Such reverence do they pay to God and his word! Let them produce even one passage from Scripture where anyone is called by name in a parable! What is meant by the words - 'There was a poor man named Lazarus?' Either the Word of God must lie, or it is a true narrative."[84]

If it were possible, I would ask Mr. Calvin that same question: what *is* meant by the words, "There was a poor man named Lazarus?" Though Lazarus' true identity has eluded theologians throughout the centuries—this is almost certainly *not* the Lazarus that Jesus raised from the dead in John's gospel—the solution may actually be found within the name itself. Lazarus' name, as it is derived from the Hebrew name *Eleazar*, meant something akin to "God is my help."[85] Perhaps the significance of calling the poor man "Lazarus" was to imply that God did what the rich man would not—help him.

This is certainly a valuable teaching point for all who suffer, specifically those who are let down by their fellow man. But since when does someone (or

---

[83] The overall case for the fictional nature of the story of Job is very sound. We have no historical evidence for the land of "Uz," and the general description that it was somewhere in the "east" (1:3) gives no hint of historical specificity. Both the prologue and the epilogue carry with them an almost storybook feel: "There lived a man named Job" who died as "an old man full of days" (1:1 and 42:17, NASB). This is eerily reminiscent of the phrases "once upon a time" and "lived happily ever after." Job also has perfect numbers of sons (7) and daughters (3), sheep (7,000) and camels (3,000), and is said to be almost unimaginably perfect and upright (1:1-8). The issue of his name even further substantiates these claims. Refer to Crenshaw's *Old Testament Wisdom* (pg. 16) for more information on the matter.

[84] John Calvin, *Tracts & Letters – Psychopannychia*.

[85] William Barclay, *The Parables of Jesus*, 92.

something) being either named or unnamed immediately determine his or her historical existence? In reality, the naming of Lazarus is no different than the aforementioned story of Job in that Job is *probably* a fictional character whose name (the "enemy," basically) implies the peculiar position that the Jewish people found themselves in during the exile; they were temporarily forsaken by God and counted as enemies.[86] For that matter, we would also have to count Eliphaz, Bildad, Zophar and Elihu as being "named" characters. On the other hand, was Job's wife not an historical person because she is unnamed? How about Noah's daughter-in-laws in the Flood account (Gen. 6-8); what were their names? Let's not get started on the number of people who are unnamed in Scripture. The door has to swing both ways. If being named equates to historicity, then being unnamed must equate to historical fiction. Lastly, if Jesus really did intend the parable of the Rich Man and Lazarus to be taken as historical truth, it is difficult to imagine why one of the two men is named and the other is left anonymous. I guess only part of the story is historically true, and the other part is fiction.

More substantial than any of this is that the historic interpretation of the parable completely disregards its obvious metaphorical claims. As one popular commentary puts it, this view ". . . ignores the element of symbolism that is quite apparent in the story. 'Abraham's side', the 'great chasm', and 'this fire' obviously ought not to be pressed into too materialistically literal a meaning, and it would be rash to attempt a description of the after-life from the details here."[87] It begins like other parables. It talks about characters that no one can actually pin down to history (even the mysterious reference to Lazarus) like other parables. On top of it all, it is probably much more imaginative and illustrative (i.e. parable-like) than any other parable in the Bible! Even if we grant that the use of the name Lazarus does somehow suggest that the story has some historical basis (at least with one character), it still cannot, by virtue of its metaphorical nature, substantiate the literal conditions of the afterlife. All of this appears to make solid logical sense, even to those (and others) that I have referenced in this section. Yet, the text

---

[86] If the dating of Job near the 6th century BCE is correct (refer back to Crenshaw, above), then other texts of the exile certainly help to substantiate the case that Job is a metaphor for Israel. For example, most of the book of Lamentations pits God and Israel as enemies, with Israel being the target of God's fury. See all of chapter two, and 3:1-18 for a strong depiction of this theme. The theme of the "enemy" saturates the texts of exile, which certainly points to the significance of Job's name.
[87] Laurence E. Porter, *New International Bible Commentary*, 1216.

continues to be one of the foundational pieces of evidence for those who uphold the TDP.

It is worth inquiring about why so many people have tended to view this particular parable differently. Why stake so much on a passage of Scripture that is, at best, highly debatable in terms of its historical veracity? To this question, I see only one plausible reason. My suggestion is that many people have not chosen to interpret this parable as historical narrative based on its actual teachings, but because it can be manipulated as evidence for a conscious state of the dead. In other words, the interpretation of the story has been skewed based on the assumption—or perhaps simply, the desire— that believers go to a place of comfort (and the wicked depart to a place of agony) immediately after death.[88] But the reasoning is completely circular, meaning that our prior beliefs influence the interpretation of a passage that is supposed to help us reach such a conclusion. While several passages of the Bible can serve as the source for this reasoning (I evaluate most of them in this book), I feel this is largely based on the fact that "tradition" tells us it is so. As I have said multiple times now: haven't we been assured that human beings "go on" as disembodied souls after death?

The fact remains that it is logically inconsistent (if not dishonest) to view the parable of the Rich Man and Lazarus as being literal, when it is functionally no different than any of the other parables we readily acknowledge as being figurative. In the end, this story carries with it tremendous meaning (as I previously discussed). Unfortunately for those who wish to wield it as evidence for a conscious, disembodied state of existence, its figurative nature simply doesn't allow that to be the meaning. While Jesus' parable of the Rich Man and Lazarus is wrought with imagery, the unusual nature of the story pales in comparison to the next one we will evaluate.

THE RETURN OF SAMUEL (AND OTHER STRANGE OCCURRENCES)

If we are being honest with ourselves—particularly with regards to the issue at hand—this is a story that no biblical scholar wants to have to explain.

---

[88] As I discuss in the final section of the book, there is always the temptation to let our own desires dictate our personal views and doctrines. In perhaps no other place is this more evident than in the issues surrounding the state of the dead and the afterlife.

Regardless of what side we may fall on concerning the state of the dead discussion, this story presents difficulties for everyone. The chief reason why this is the case is that the raising of Samuel's spirit has no genuine parallel anywhere in the Bible; nowhere else do we see a disembodied human being conjured up from the dead, much less one that can interact with the living. Needless to say, this is one of the strangest and most intriguing stories in the entire Bible. In fairness, its unusual nature is probably why the story is not used more frequently to support notions of the afterlife. Still, it may actually have some bearing on what will happen to each of us at death.

For those who are not familiar with the story, it is found in 1 Samuel 28. In this chapter of the book, we see a terrified Saul at the lowest point of his failure as Israel's first king. The Philistines are closing in, and he is quickly losing favor with the people and with God. Out of sheer desperation, Saul asks a female conjurer from a place called Endor to raise the spirit of Samuel from the dead. Since Samuel was a great prophet of God and his former counselor, Saul figures that Samuel is his last resort for advice in his time of need. Shockingly, the "witch of Endor" successfully raises Samuel's spirit from the dead, and Saul is able to communicate with him once more.

Unfortunately for Saul, the counsel he would receive offered him little consolation. Instead, Samuel gives him a grave prophecy: "The Lord will deliver both Israel and you into the hands of the Philistines, and tomorrow you and your sons will be with me. The Lord will also give the army of Israel into the hands of the Philistines" (v. 19). After this pronouncement, Samuel mysteriously leaves the scene. Some ancient rabbinic texts suggest that *Samuel* was the one who was terrified by the whole ordeal because he feared that he was being summoned to appear before God for the final judgment.[89] This would make some sense being that the predominant biblical view is that the great Day of Judgment is the next step after death, not conscious existence as a disembodied soul. As far as where Samuel went after his meeting with Saul, however, we know nothing. Much like Satan in the book of Job, he simply vanishes from the text.

As previously mentioned, neither testament of the Bible mentions anyone else who was ever conjured from the dead in such a way. The Old Testament tells us that both Elijah and Elisha raised people from the dead,[90] and someone was raised merely by touching Elisha's bones (2 Ki. 13:21).

---

[89] "Samuel," *JewishEncyclopedia.com*.
[90] 1 Kings 17:21-22, 2 Kings 4:34-35.

The New Testament does record the fact that Lazarus (Jn. 11:38-44), Jairus' daughter (Mk. 5:22-43, Lk. 8:41-56), a widow's son (Lk. 7:11-17), a woman named Dorcas (Acts 9:40), and a man named Eutychus (Acts 20:9-10) were all raised back to life. While all were indeed resurrected, my point can be made in evaluating the first two of these resurrection accounts.

The opening couple of points to consider is that these events were accomplished by Jesus rather than by a pagan medium, and each was significantly different than the conjuring of Samuel's spirit; both individuals were brought back to life as they previously existed, meaning that they came back in bodily form. These events certainly serve as substantial evidence of Jesus' divine authority, but they are also rather intriguing within the scope of this book. If both individuals ventured to a more preferable existence in the intermediate state,[91] then how should we view their resurrections? Apparently, they were called back from their blissful lives as disembodied spirits, just so they could be placed into an inferior existence within their earthly bodies. This being the case, it is rather strange that both examples are celebrated as being great and miraculous events.

In the minds of those who bore witness to these resurrections, Jesus had given them an astonishing gift—they had once more been given life. But I have tremendous difficulties in understanding how these resurrections can be viewed so positively if they were indeed living in a more preferable state before that. While those around them were certainly amazed (Lk. 8:56), I cannot help but feel that Lazarus and the young girl would have lamented their circumstances. Perhaps they would have thought to themselves: "Thanks a lot for bringing us back here, Jesus. Not only were we robbed of a better existence, but we have to die all over again!" Predictably, the chief priests almost immediately made a plot to kill Lazarus after his resurrection (Jn. 12:9-11). If the two were living in peace and comfort as immaterial spirits, then Jesus would actually have been doing them a disservice. Furthermore, it is specifically mentioned that Lazarus' death caused great distress for nearly everyone around him—including Jesus, who famously "wept" (Jn. 11:35)—and the emotional ramifications were obvious (11:31-33). It is strange that even Jesus himself viewed Lazarus' passing as a tragic event, since Jesus

---

[91] Supporters of the *temporary-disembodiment position* (the TDP) assert that the intermediate state, however hazy it may be, is still superior to our lives here on earth. See chapter four, "Just Add Body."

should have believed (according to many Christian traditions) that Lazarus was now in a "better place."

Finally, none of the texts that recorded these resurrection events mention a *single* word about the person's experience in heaven or Abraham's bosom. This particular omission is rather telling because we should expect to hear at least something about their experiences, if they had indeed visited either of the aforementioned places. In fact, not one of these people came back speaking about the afterlife; not Lazarus, not Eutychus, not Dorcas, not the young girl, and not those who were raised by either Elijah or Elisha. This does not tell us to a certainty that they didn't go to a conscious, intermediate realm at death. But it does at least mean that the biblical authors didn't have anything of the sort to report in any of these instances. I realize that it's not usually wise to make an argument from silence. That is, unless, we are dealing with a powerful silence. I believe that all of these points merge to create an interesting problem for temporary-disembodiment proponents. In these cases, it simply makes much better sense to believe that death marked the cessation of conscious life rather than the immediate continuation of a more preferable disembodied existence.

Besides these examples, the Bible certainly discusses the appearance of others who had passed away. However, none of these examples are about disembodied spirits returning to earth. Jesus himself was raised with a tangible body, and the first of the resurrection bodies at that (1 Cor. 15:23). Elijah and Moses both appeared at the Transfiguration, as mentioned in the synoptic gospels.[92] Elijah was specifically mentioned as being taken directly to heaven as a unique event (2 Ki. 2:1-12), so his presence there is not quite as difficult to understand; we know for certain that he was already there. We also know that he was "assumed" into heaven, meaning that he had been taken in bodily form prior to death. Another reason for Elijah's appearance was that many Jews had come to believe that Elijah would return to the world before the messiah would arrive.[93] His appearance at the Transfiguration, then, was another testament to the fact that the messiah had indeed come in Jesus.

Similarly, Moses' presence at the event also testified to the fact that

---

[92] The synoptic gospels include Matthew, Mark, and Luke. The word "synoptic" literally breaks down to something like "seen together." These three gospels share so many similarities that they are grouped, or "seen," as one unit.

[93] This particular tradition is clear within the writings of the New Testament itself. Matthew 16:14, Mark 8:28, and Luke 9:19 all mention the idea that some believed that Jesus was really Elijah.

Jesus was indeed the long-awaited messiah. Just as Moses had received the instructions for the old covenant on a mountain (Sinai) in the presence of God, he was there to hand off the reigns of the new covenant on another mountain; but this time, he was in the presence of God incarnate. We know that Moses was laid to rest just prior to the Israelite conquest of Canaan (Dt. 34:5), and all the Bible provides about his existence afterwards is an odd reference from the book of Jude that suggests that Michael (an archangel) once battled Satan over his body (1:9). While interpretations vary, this passage gives no hint that Moses existed in a disembodied form after his death. In fact, it suggests this was an issue revolving around Moses' physical existence.[94] Like Paul's heavenly experience in 2 Corinthians 12:1-5, Moses' presence at the Transfiguration certainly cannot stand as evidence that all believers go to heaven when they die. The Transfiguration was clearly a miraculous (and isolated) event in the ministry of Jesus.

In any case, neither Moses nor Elijah arrived as immaterial beings. If we remember, Peter asked Jesus if the apostles should build shelters for those who were present at the Transfiguration.[95] This would suggest that Jesus, Elijah, and Moses were present in bodily form; an immaterial spirit doesn't need a shelter! Like those who came out of the tombs in Matthew 27 (which I discuss momentarily), we simply do not know what types of bodies Moses and Elijah possessed at that point; but they did have bodies. To be consistent with my overall position, it is as reasonable as any other view (if not more so) to posit that both individuals had been transformed into angelic form. Both men enjoyed special privileges because of their roles in the Old Testament narrative. In summary, there are two major points to consider about Moses and Elijah's presence at the Transfiguration. The first is that both men were there for the express purpose of validating that Jesus was the messiah, as a sort of inauguration event. The second point is that both of them also appeared in embodied form, which does *anything* but lend credibility to the idea that there is a disembodied interim period.

While we are talking about one of the only two people in the entire Bible who were taken directly to heaven, it is worth mentioning that these miraculous events are rather telling in the greater discussion of the afterlife.

---

[94] There is an apocryphal tradition that Moses' body was assumed into heaven after Michael and Satan fought over his body. See Wheaton's article in the *New Bible Commentary*, 1418.

[95] Matthew 17:4, Mark 9:5 and Luke 9:33.

These occasions were special circumstances in which two righteous men (Elijah and Enoch) were able to bypass death entirely in order to live with God in heaven. The very reason that these two circumstances are considered to be so special is that neither Elijah nor Enoch had to share in the common fate of all other human beings; they never had to die before entering into a blissful existence with God (if the Jewish people of those days even believed in a universal afterlife, that is).[96] If all fallen believers go directly to heaven at death, then the stories of Elijah and Enoch cease to be truly distinct events. At the least, these events certainly lose much of their luster. This is especially true when we consider that they were taken body and all (i.e. "assumed"), whereas we would simply be taken in spirit form. These accounts, in and of themselves, actually pose a problem to the idea that all believers venture to heaven after death. These events are clearly not evidence in favor of the TDP.

Returning to the main point, we should also consider the case of those who were released from their tombs after the Crucifixion (Mt. 27:52-53). These were apparently people who were dead in their tombs, awaiting resurrection. On this note, it is important to consider that those emerging from the tombs were described as "bodies" (*somata*). This would have been an excellent time to refer to them as "spirits" or "souls," if Matthew had actually intended it to be understood that way. It is probably most logical to believe that these people came back with their earthly bodies—just as Lazarus had, for example—because it is clear that Jesus received the first of the resurrection bodies (1 Cor. 15:23, 44-49), and Jesus had not been raised at this point in Matthew's narrative.

We can wonder what type of bodies they may have had, given that many could have been decomposed by then, but the text lends no support for the idea that these were disembodied spirits who consciously existed prior to that time. The purpose of the event is probably much like those of Moses and Elijah's presence at the Transfiguration, or the incredible display of different languages (tongues) at the day of Pentecost (Acts 2:3-4), or the tearing of the temple vale (Mt. 27:51) after the Crucifixion; these were inauguration events that were intended to display the reality that God's Kingdom had broken into the world. As such, they do not speak to the norm of the Christian experience

---

[96] The Jewish belief in the afterlife was almost certainly undeveloped in both Enoch and Elijah's respective time periods. The apocalyptic movement, which largely began in the exilic/post-exilic period and went through the period of the New Testament, added a great deal of depth to the subject.

any more than Elijah's trip to heaven does. To think they do is similar to believing that everyone who withholds money from the church or swears a false oath to God will be struck down on the spot (Acts 5:1-11). Clearly, that is not the case.

The key with the examples mentioned here is that they are exceptions to the rule and not the rule itself. By now, it is probably becoming apparent that biblical exceptions are perhaps the main source of evidence for the belief that we consciously live somewhere during the interim period. Suffice it to say that, beyond the odd case of Samuel, there aren't any other genuine examples involving the appearance of human spirits from the grave. All other instances involve embodied individuals; they are not "naked spirits," as is proposed in the TDP. Moses, Elijah, and those who were released from their tombs after the Crucifixion are all described as appearing in some type of bodily form. For all of these reasons, the conjuring of Samuel's spirit should not be used by anyone as evidence of our existence in the interim period. To do so would be to invite a plethora of additional questions that would need explaining.

As obscure as this passage is within our conversation about the state of the dead, and within the entire canon of Scripture for that matter, it is still both interesting and beneficial for us to examine. To add context to the story, consider that Saul had recently banished all of the "mediums and spiritists" from Israel (1 Sam. 28:3). While the text doesn't directly tell us why he chose to do so, we do know that such practices were strictly forbidden in Jewish law well before that time (Lev. 19:31, 20:6). The surrounding nations like Mesopotamia and Sumer were somewhat fascinated by the practice of necromancy (summoning or communicating with the dead), but Israel was not permitted to participate in such things. In fact, the practices of necromancy and ancestor worship were considered by the Jewish people to be closely connected to the belief in the continuous life of the soul (i.e. the immortality of the soul).[97] Surprise, surprise.

The previous points raise some interesting questions. First and foremost, why is it that God banned Israel from attempting to communicate with the dead to begin with? It could not merely be that other nations engaged in these practices. Some actually speculate that this prohibition proves that Israel must have believed in the validity of necromancy (that it is at least possible to contact that dead),[98] but there is a problem with this logic. If such a thing

---

[97] "Immortality of the Soul," JewishEncyclopedia.com.

[98] J.P. Moreland and Scott B. Rae, *Body & Soul*, 28.

were possible, what would be the harm in seeking counsel via fallen prophets (like Samuel) or searching for comfort by speaking to deceased loved ones? There doesn't seem to be any logical reason why God should forbid such a thing, and we aren't given any direct textual reason why this was the case.

Both Leviticus 19:31 and 20:6 suggest that entertaining mediums would be a source of "defilement" and spiritual "prostitution," but this just moves the goal posts back even further; we still aren't told *why* this would be the case. Given the Old Testament perspectives concerning the unity of the body and the soul, it stands to reason that divination and necromancy were forbidden because God knew that such efforts would not actually lead to communication with dead *people* at all. As I explain in chapter five, the Bible does not suggest (much less promote) that possibility. Rather, it is quite logical to believe that such attempts are actually legitimate ways to invite demonic entities into our lives. This would make sense of the fact that a seemingly innocent practice (contacting grandma) was so sternly discouraged within the Jewish culture. Furthermore, the Bible speaks of demonic entities repeatedly, but never again speaks of the actual existence of ghosts or the spirits of the dead contacting the living.

What does this have to do with our discussion about the state of the dead and Samuel's spirit? Well, it certainly means that Saul was doing something that was not only forbidden, but probably impossible. More germane to our conversation, it may also mean that the "spirit of Samuel" wasn't really Samuel at all. If it were, then we would have to explain why this is the only example of such a thing in the entire Bible, why it flies in the face of nearly every other biblical description about the state of the dead, and why a pagan medium was actually able to accomplish the feat of raising Samuel's spirit from the grave. It would be consistent that such a person could perhaps conjure a demonic entity through her practices, but raising the spirit of a renowned man of Yahweh is an entirely different issue altogether. This would certainly be a "house divided," so to speak. Furthermore, we have the problem that a manifestation of this variety should be impossible based on the biblical concepts of body/soul unity. While not directly related, we are also left to wonder the reasons for Samuel's abrupt and mysterious disappearance. This is a very strange story indeed!

On a final note, this passage contains a specific detail that directly speaks to the issues surrounding the state of the dead. Let's recall Samuel's statement to Saul regarding his impending doom: ". . . tomorrow you and your sons will be with me" (v. 19). On the one hand, we have Samuel, the faithful follower of

God and well-respected prophet. On the other, we have Saul, the murderous, idolatrous, unfaithful king of Israel who would later impale himself (1 Sam. 31:4, 1 Chron. 10:4). If we hold to the view that Samuel was living somewhere as a disembodied spirit, such as the "Abraham's bosom" we later hear about in the New Testament, prior to being raised, then we have a serious problem on our hands.

Why would the good prophet Samuel and the corrupt king Saul both be sent to the same location upon their deaths? Since it clearly wasn't based on their religious faithfulness, there is only one logical solution to the problem: when Samuel (assuming it was him) told Saul that he and his sons will "be with (him) tomorrow," Samuel was clearly not referring to a conscious, intermediate realm for the dead. Instead, he must have been referring to Sheol, which is simply the abode of the dead. In other words, Samuel was lying dead (unconsciously) prior to being raised, and Saul and his sons would be doing the same the following day. Given all of these points, it should be clear that the account of the witch of Endor raising Samuel's spirit from the dead is a biblical anomaly that does not get us far in understanding where *we* go directly after death. That is, unless, we acknowledge the basic teaching that we all go to the grave. However, the text may be of more use to those who wish to talk about the powers of darkness and the dangers of attempting to contact the dead. I will talk about both of these issues in the last chapter of the book.

DESCENDING INTO HELL

I believe in God the Father Almighty, Maker of heaven and earth.

And in Jesus Christ his only Son our Lord; who was conceived by the Holy Ghost, born of the Virgin Mary, suffered under Pontius Pilate, was crucified, dead, and buried; he descended into hell; the third day he rose again from the dead; he ascended into heaven, and sitteth on the right hand of God the Father Almighty; from thence he shall come to judge the quick and the dead.

I believe in the Holy Ghost; the holy catholic Church; the communion of saints; the forgiveness of sins; the resurrection of the body; and the life everlasting. Amen.

The Apostles' Creed (shown above)—as well as the later Athanasian Creed—has often been taken to suggest that Jesus ventured to the underworld after his death on the cross.[99] This belief developed over time into what is now frequently referred to as the "Harrowing of Hell," in which Jesus is believed to have liberated the souls who were living in the underworld prior to his resurrection. The idea is that the time between Christ's death and resurrection was occupied by a disembodied journey to the realm of the dead. During that time, Jesus would have announced all of the wonderful truths about his ministry to the saints of old. He would have preached about the Incarnation, the Atonement, the realization of the long-awaited messiah, as well as the future events surrounding the Parousia (the second "coming"). In doing so, the saints who were living on the "sunny side" of the underworld would have been liberated to heaven. In this sense, we can think of Christ as having personally taken atonement back to the religious faithful of the past. Based on these viewpoints, the Harrowing of Hell could be used as evidence for the belief in a conscious interim period, wherein disembodied human souls await Christ's coming and the reception of their new bodies. Though Christ's supposed trip to the underworld has become part of the history of biblical interpretation, the question remains as to whether or not it is biblically grounded to begin with. We now turn our attention to answering that very question.

One of the more intriguing biblical passages that gave rise to the belief in the Harrowing of Hell is found in Paul's letter to the Ephesians. In 4:7-10, we read a rather perplexing message about Christ's "gift" to believers:

> "But to each one of us grace has been given as Christ apportioned it. This is why it says: 'When he ascended on high, he took many captives and gave gifts to his people.' (What does 'he ascended' mean except that he also descended to the lower, earthly regions? He who descended is the very one who ascended higher than all the heavens, in order to fill the whole universe.)"

---

[99] The early church creeds are essentially concise articles that are supposed to express the essential elements of the Christian faith. As such, they were intended to reflect the biblical teachings on a variety of matters. Among the issues often taken up within the creeds are things like the nature of the Trinity, the purpose of baptism, confirmation of the collective church body, and the affirmation of key principles like the resurrection of Jesus and the second coming.

This passage seems to suggest some very important things within the confines of this particular topic. The first point is that Christ apparently took others with him when he ascended back to heaven; he "led a host of captives" when he returned. Who these captives actually were is another matter altogether. Are we talking about every believer of the past, or just particular ones? While the ascension of Christ is clearly being referenced, the more interesting aspect of the text has to do with where Jesus ascended *from*. In Paul's line of reasoning, the Ascension is rightly termed as such because Christ had previously descended into the "lower regions, the earth." This terminology is represented, whether correctly or incorrectly, in the aforementioned Apostles' and Athanasian Creeds.

When we look around the New Testament a bit, we find only a couple other references to something that even resembles this event, both of which come from the first letter of Peter. In 1 Peter 3:18-20, we hear about the triumphant nature of Christ's victory over death. In verse 19, it is said that Jesus went to proclaim victory to the "imprisoned spirits." This phrase has proven to be rather enigmatic since its inception some two thousand years ago, but we do know from the text itself a little about who these imprisoned spirits were. This is perhaps a reference to those beings who did not obey God in the days that Noah was building the ark, in anticipation of the coming flood.

In a less ambiguous way, 1 Peter 4:6 makes mention of a similar belief: "For this is the reason the gospel was preached even to those who are now dead, so that they might be judged according to human standards in regard to the body, but live according to God in regard to the spirit." Again, there are many possible meanings here.[100] It makes a great deal of sense that the reference is to Christians that were judged by the earthly courts and executed, but would nevertheless be raised at the end by the Spirit.[101] Though it is a bit more theologically palatable, the exact meaning of this verse still eludes any positive identification. We simply do not know, with any degree of certainty, the identity of these people. For obvious reasons, few interpreters use any of these passages as evidence for the norm of Christian life after death. Like Samuel's return, there are a number of difficulties that must first be explained in order to use them in such a way.

---

[100] For a further discussion of the possibilties, see Wayne Grudem's, *The First Epistle of Peter*, 170-172.

[101] Craig S. Keener, *The IVP Bible Background Commentary*, 719.

Naturally, if the Harrowing of Hell really occurred, it could suggest that disembodied spirits can actually exist in the first place. This is questionable in and of itself, and the basic premise of this book is that such a thing is not biblically plausible when all of the factors are considered. *Even if* something like this did take place, the biggest problem is that there is nothing to suggest that those who were liberated during this time were consciously living in the underworld. This is absolutely crucial. In this sense, these passages are eerily reminiscent of the one dealt with in the previous section concerning those who emerged from their tombs (Mt. 27:52). For all we know, the passages that gave rise to the Harrowing of Hell could simply be implying that Jesus brought the reality of his atonement to those who were in the realm of the dead. In other words, it is a metaphorical way of relating the fact that Christ had conquered the grave and that his victory had very real effects on those who had departed.

The terminology employed within the creeds simply reflects the idea that Christ descended to the "lower regions" (*katōtera merē*), as Ephesians 4:9 puts it, after his death. It's worth noting that nothing in the creeds or the Bible itself states that Jesus travelled to hell (Gehenna) or some conscious abode of the dead; he simply "descended" into the "lower regions." It is only assumed that those who were waiting there were *consciously* awaiting their liberation, so it is at least equally probable that Christ ventured to the place described within the Bible's truest teachings about the "underworld"—the grave.

The biblical concepts of Sheol and Hades, at the base level, simply refer to the place where dead people go. It was largely the Greek philosophers of the day who began to think of Hades as a labyrinth for conscious souls. These are the same people, mind you, who generally aligned with the philosophical belief that the human soul was its own immortal being, and that it awaited release from the inferior body. Interestingly enough, even those who support the TDP are quick to point out that Sheol, for example, is best characterized as an *unconscious* state of being. Scott B. Rae and J.P. Moreland, both theologians and philosophers, verify this point in their very first argument that Sheol represents a conscious place of existence for the soul.[102] Even those who view Sheol as a conscious existence are forced to admit that the Old Testament

---

[102] In an exceptionally odd way of proving that the interim period is a conscious one, they say: "First, life in Sheol is often depicted as lethargic, inactive and resembling an unconscious coma (Job 3:13, Ps. 88:10-12, 115:17-18, Ecc. 9:10, Is. 38:18)." Clearly, this is actually evidence *against* their position. Moreland and Rae, *Body and Soul*, 32.

often describes it in precisely the opposite way. With all of this being said, Jesus certainly did travel to the "lower regions" when he died because he went into the earth (metaphorically), and the earth is where the dead return. Once again, these passages need not reflect the notion of an immaterial underworld in which the spirits of deceased people consciously exist.

As this section draws to a close, we are prepared to conclude our discussion about the Harrowing of Hell. There are unquestionable difficulties in dealing with the passages that discuss Christ's activities after the Crucifixion, but the issue still comes down to the collective biblical evidence on the matter. Whether Christ truly "harrowed the underworld," or simply "harrowed the grave," will hinge upon how we view the rest of the materials available to us. Whatever the case, these passages simply do not provide us with an explanation about what happens to each of us when we die. Jesus may have gone to retrieve all of the old covenant believers of the past, or just significant figures like David and Abraham. Then again, this may have been referring to certain fallen angelic beings, which is a possible interpretation of 1 Peter 3:19, or to something different altogether.

More importantly, Jesus may only have gone to the grave, and the previous passages are intended to imply that salvation extended back to those who looked forward to the messiah in the Old Testament. While we should not doubt that something of the sort happened after the Crucifixion—this reality is clearly mentioned several times within the New Testament—the truth is that we cannot be sure of what all this event entailed. For these reasons, it does not get us much farther than the story of Samuel does in terms of determining the post-mortem condition of believers.

A FOOT IN EACH DOOR

At the onset of this chapter, I mentioned that thinkers often attempt to fit all of the biblical passages that speak to the afterlife together into one tidy group. This point is well worth revisiting at the close of this chapter. If one is to believe that the Harrowing of Hell provides evidence for a conscious, disembodied realm of the dead—or that any passage of the Bible does, for that matter—then it cannot also be held that we immediately go to heaven or hell when we die. This is precisely the problem I addressed concerning Jesus and his dealings with the criminal on the cross. The crucial point here is that we cannot have it both ways. We cannot smuggle in some mixture of views about the afterlife and keep all of our ducks in a row, so to speak. It is just as apologist Greg Koukl said when he considered whether or not all views of the afterlife can be true at once: "When you die, maybe you go to heaven or hell. Maybe you get reincarnated . . . Maybe you lie in the grave. But you can't do them all at the same time."[103]

Temporary-disembodiment proponents are particularly guilty of this, as they often use diverging lines of reasoning to support the overall belief that the soul consciously survives the death of the body. In this, the passages suggesting that the deceased may immaterially dwell somewhere like Abraham's bosom, Hades, Sheol, or the like, are heaped together with those that suggest we may go directly to heaven or hell. Maybe the soul does consciously depart to one of these realms when we die, but it certainly won't be heading to all of them. One simply cannot say that all of these locations are possible destinations during the interim period because we would no longer have a coherent view of the issue. Temporary-disembodiment proponents cannot take every possible suggestion about the state of the dead and combine them to prove a *particular view* on the issue. If a text is interpreted as discussing a conscious interim existence in heaven, then it cannot also be taken as evidence that we go to Abraham's bosom. The same applies to hell (Gehenna) and Hades. As I have said repeatedly throughout this book, these are all different realms or locations.

As a way of easily understanding what I am trying to say, consider the following analogy. A woman (we'll call her *Jan*) is suspected of murdering her husband. As the police begin to investigate her, they first attempt to ascertain her whereabouts on the date and time in question (*June 25th near 3:00 p.m.*, we'll say). As they interview those who could possibly substantiate an alibi for Jan, the case takes a difficult turn for the investigators. On the one hand, a neighbor reported that she saw Jan in town at the local movie theatre around 3:00 p.m. on the day in question. Shortly thereafter, Jan's brother notified detectives that she was actually out of town visiting him on the day in question. If either person is telling the truth, then Jan could not have been home to murder her husband at that exact time. The problem is that we have conflicting reports about Jan's whereabouts. Does the fact that both people placed Jan away from her home on the date and time in question actually substantiate that she was indeed somewhere else? The answer, of course, is no. Rather, this simply tells us that there are conflicting reports

---

[103] Greg Koukl, "The Intolerance of Tolerance."

concerning Jan's whereabouts at that time. If anything, the case has actually become more complicated. It could be that one of the witnesses is telling the truth, or it could be that neither of them are telling the truth. But it cannot be that both of them are accurately describing her whereabouts. *Jan cannot be in two places at the same time.*

The point of this analogy should be clear. We cannot use passages that suggest our souls will venture to heaven or hell at death along with passages that suggest that the human soul passes to another realm (like Hades or Abraham's bosom) as common evidence for the TDP. We are dealing with two very different realities, and we certainly cannot have a foot in each door. As it stands, temporary-disembodiment proponents look a lot like the scarecrow on the *Wizard of Oz* when he first met Dorothy; while instructing us on which way to go, they confidently point in opposite directions. My position, which I hope will continue to appear more plausible as we progress into the following chapters, is that neither line of reasoning is actually correct. We do not go to heaven or hell, Hades or Sheol, or anywhere else, as conscious, disembodied spirits.

With this being said, I do not want us to lose the power of the point I am trying to make in this section of the book. Attempting to combine divergent lines of thinking is a fallacy that few interpreters (if any) have acknowledged, and it is utterly devastating to the TDP. As I pointed out in chapter two, the attempt to use near-death experiences to prove any *specific* Christian doctrine of the afterlife proves unsuccessful for identical reasons. Scholars have either failed to realize this particular problem or, worse, have attempted to conceal it. Based on the amount of theological contortion involved in the TDP, I fear that the latter may often be true. With this conundrum in place, we are now prepared to move on to discuss what I feel are the strongest objections against the belief in a conscious state of the dead, and the rest of the evidence in favor of my view of the interim period.

CHAPTER FOUR

THE DEATH BLOW

To this point, I have mainly evaluated the sections of Scripture that are often understood to promote the immediacy of the afterlife and a conscious interim period. Any such view supports, in some way or another, the belief in the immortality of the soul and the *temporary-disembodiment position* (the TDP). To again clarify these perspectives, the most common Christian view of the afterlife is that the soul is temporarily able to consciously exist apart from the body after death. It is thought that we (our souls, really) can enter into an intermediate state of consciousness between our deaths and resurrections. Within the TDP, there is the possibility of life in two different categories of existence. All deceased individuals will live in either 1) heaven or hell, or 2) Abraham's bosom or Sheol/Hades. While hell is the final abode of the wicked, none of these other destinations is what the Bible consistently portrays as our ultimate hope for the afterlife; the goal is a new body, where we will live in the new heavens and new earth.

While the Bible does not provide an enormous wealth of detail about the state of the dead, the teachings we do have are not particularly supportive of any temporary-disembodiment perspective. In fact, some of them appear to contradict such a notion when thoroughly examined. One of the main passages where Jesus is supposedly supporting a conscious disembodied existence (the parable of the Rich Man and Lazarus) cannot be taken literally; to do so would reveal an inconsistent and biased method of biblical interpretation. Likewise, Jesus' discussion with the criminal on the cross turns in drastic directions (at least temporally) based on a plethora of factors, and this is widely recognized by almost any honest biblical scholar. More than that, it is completely reasonable to believe that Jesus' intention was to tell the criminal that he would indeed be in "paradise"—meaning the consummated Kingdom of God, in that context—upon its arrival.

While extremely fascinating, the story of Samuel's mysterious appearance from the dead offers more questions than solutions. Finally, Paul's statements about being "in our out" of the "flesh," "body," or "tent" lend themselves to a number of possibilities. Given Paul's firm stance against views of soul superiority (as seen in 1 Cor. 15, for example), it would be odd that he would provide us with something that is the functional equivalent: i.e. souls consciously existing somewhere without the need of a body. Just to make this clear—it is terribly hard to imagine that Paul would so adamantly oppose those who desired to live without a body, only to advance a similar argument himself. Given the notable room for interpretation within these passages, you may wonder where to go from here. How exactly do we deal with such uncertainty?

When faced with passages that do not lend themselves to obvious conclusions, we are wise to press on to others that are less ambiguous. This is how any good interpretive practice is supposed to operate, regardless of what issue we are talking about. In the first chapter of the book, I discussed two of these more concrete passages of Scripture (1 Cor. 15 and 1 Thes. 4:13-18) that tell us much about the nature of the afterlife. Over the course of the last two chapters, I have addressed those passages of Scripture that are most frequently used in support of a conscious, disembodied existence during the interim period—the time between our deaths and the reception of our new bodies at the resurrection. Along the way, I showed that more "traditional" interpretations of these passages face a number of interpretive difficulties, and that viewing the interim period as an unconscious state of being makes the best sense of the collective biblical evidence. The final push—or *death blow*—for my view of the afterlife is a series of biblical and logical arguments that I feel are extremely difficult to explain away. When these arguments are placed together with the previous sections of the book, my hope is that it will become apparent that the soul cannot go on to consciously and independently dwell somewhere else when we die. At the same time, these objections cast further doubt on the TDP. Ultimately, I believe that what follows is simply too much for the TDP to withstand.

SATAN'S DOMAIN

The belief in hell can be plainly seen within every part of orthodox Christianity, from the biblical texts themselves, to the pulpits of most denominational backgrounds. Though the belief that the unrepentant will be sentenced to hell is roughly as old as the belief that the righteous will live with God for the rest of eternity, there is much disagreement on its particulars.[104] For our purposes, the details of hell largely have to do with timing. Specifically, we must seek to understand *when* hell will become the dwelling place for the unrepentant. In doing so, we may actually shed some light on when believers will experience the unimaginable bliss of the new heavens and new earth. That is, it would be difficult to hold that the dead in Christ immediately go to heaven if the lost do not go directly to hell. As I will explain, the Bible places the separation of the righteous and the wicked—and their appropriate placements—together as a simultaneous event.

In evaluating the temporal aspects of hell, it will actually be necessary to first discuss its most prominent figure. Of all the topics presented within the vast world of apocalyptic literature, perhaps none have captivated the minds of people from all creeds and backgrounds more than the character we commonly refer to as "Satan." We know him as the *evil one, the Devil,* the *adversary* of God and man, the one who commands a legion of fallen angels . . . and *the one who is destined for the "pit" and the fiery bottoms of hell.* While all of this is at some level biblically accurate, there are a plethora of misconceptions about Satan drifting around the world. This is even (if not especially) true within the church. Of equal importance is the fact that Satan's existence, and his ultimate doom, can actually tell us quite a lot about our future as well. While he is often viewed as being the ruler of hell, this is only true (and partially, at that) in the greater, eschatological sense. This means that if Satan is not *currently* in hell, then we may be urged to change our views about when anyone will exist there.

In the Old Testament, there is relatively little discussion about Satan or demonic entities. To some, this is rather surprising considering the fact that he is so pervasive within the minds of even modern men and women. Satan's first appearance within the Bible is almost immediate, as he is viewed in the form of a serpent that subtly convinces Adam and Eve to forsake the one prohibition that God actually gave them (Gen. 3:1-6). Though the text only refers to this stealthy creature as "the serpent," later theological perspectives would identify the serpent and Satan as one in the same (Jn. 8:44, Rev. 20:2):

---

[104] For a good assessment of the ways one might view the nature of hell, I recommend *Four Views on Hell,* for both its brevity and its portrayal of the debate that has occurred over this issue.

if not in form, then at least in spirit. Not surprisingly, he is known as the "tempter," for he enticed Adam and Eve to disobey God. As theologically weighty as Adam and Eve's rebellion is within the biblical narrative—considering that it was *the* event that brought sin into the world and sparked an entire age of turmoil and spiritual battle—the biggest surprise is how rarely Satan is mentioned in the Old Testament afterwards. For all intents and purposes, the serpent disappears for a rather long period of time. After Genesis 3, there is no genuine discussion of Satan throughout the rest of the Pentateuch (the first five books of the Bible), and virtually no discussion of him in either the historical or prophetic works. Where did he go?

Satan's most noteworthy appearance in the remainder of the Old Testament is within the book of Job, where the name "Satan," meaning "the adversary," is actually coined. As in the Garden of Eden, Satan serves the role of the being who attempts to turn humanity against its Creator. But Satan is not quite as successful with Job as he was with Adam and Eve. Among its many timeless teachings, the book of Job reveals the fact that Satan appears to have fully resurfaced in Jewish thought near the time of the exile. At the least, the Jews began to view him as an even fiercer adversary than they had previously imagined. The great prophet Isaiah gives us some early aliases just prior to, or very near to, the exile; "In that day, the Lord will punish with his sword—his fierce, great and powerful sword—Leviathan the gliding serpent, Leviathan the coiling serpent; he will slay the monster of the sea" (27:1). While apocalyptic thought was building, so too was the belief that Satan is the enemy of God and his people. With the incarnation of the Son of God in the man Jesus, we would finally see the Devil for who he really is.

In the New Testament, information about Satan and the powers of darkness seem to burst out of the text. This makes a lot of sense, being that the Son of God had taken up human form with his creation; the closer God gets, the more defensive His enemies become. Nowhere is this more apparent than in those instances when demons actually sense Jesus' presence from afar. In Mark 5:1-7, for example, a legion of demons appears to understand the divine power of Christ before he even addresses them. It is also in the New Testament that Satan is given dozens of different names, and is said to have offered Jesus all of the kingdoms of the world if he would leave the purpose of the cross behind (Mt. 4:1-11). Later on, we see Jesus refer to Peter as "Satan" because he was also attempting to create a cross-less messiah who didn't really need to die for the sins of the world (Mt. 16:23). Furthermore, we receive Jesus' own personal account of Satan's astonishing fall from grace, in which he proclaimed that he saw Satan ". . . fall like lightning from the heavens" (Lk. 10:18). In the book of Revelation, it is revealed that the "dragon" (another one of Satan's aliases) will gather together all of those who follow him for one final attempt to do the impossible—defeat God and His angels:

> "When the thousand years are over, Satan will be released
> from his prison and will go out to deceive the nations in
> the four corners of the earth—Gog and Magog—and to
> gather them for battle. In number they are like the sand on
> the seashore. They marched across the breadth of the earth
> and surrounded the camp of God's people, the city he loves.
> But fire came down from heaven and devoured them. And
> the devil, who deceived them, was thrown into the lake of
> burning sulfur, where the beast and the false prophet had
> been thrown. They will be tormented day and night for ever
> and ever."[105]

Finally, and perhaps most importantly (as far as this book is concerned), it is for Satan and his minions that hell is actually created in the first place (Mt. 25:41). As interesting as it is to discuss Satan's background and his identity, we are now beginning to get somewhere with regards to our discussion of the afterlife. Within the biblical text, Satan's impact on the world is overwhelming. He is present in the most important events of the biblical narrative: from the Fall, to Jesus' path towards the cross, to the very "end of the age" itself. Given his overwhelming presence within this world, we arrive at a very intriguing question: if Satan has his hands all over the events of this world, how can he dwell in hell?

If the Bible—particularly the New Testament—tells us anything about Satan, it is that he is able to impact *this world* at *this time*. Satan is not in hell torturing Adolph Hitler and Ted Bundy with whips and chains. On that note, he never will be doing such a thing. That kind of talk is just pure folklore. Centuries before the coming of Christ, the book of Job revealed the belief that Satan surveys the world in search of people to deceive (1:6-7). We see precisely the same type of thinking in the New Testament. This is perhaps most apparent in a text like 1 Peter 5:8; "Be alert and of sober mind. Your

---

[105] Revelation 20:7-10.

enemy the devil prowls around like a roaring lion looking for someone to devour." While some Christians understand this point, it may come as quite a surprise to others. After all, some of the most pervasive images we see of this fallen angel are associated with him being the ruler of hell. Medieval literature is full of terrifying images of Satan and his legion of demons dragging horrified sinners to their destruction beneath the earth.[106]

Certainly, all of this is both fascinating and thought provoking. The problem is that it isn't even close to being an accurate biblical portrayal of reality. Biblically speaking, this point is irrefutable: never once does the Bible suggest that Satan is presently in hell. We see him in the Garden, in the mysterious land of Uz, in the heavenly realm as he reports to God, at the beginning of Jesus' ministry, and eventually at the end of the age as he attempts to battle Christ and the heavenly army, *but never do we see him in hell.* Likewise, it should not come as a shock that all demonic activity is also kept within the bounds of either this world or the heavens. Jesus cast a demon out of a man in the Jewish synagogue (Lk. 4:31-37), a "legion" of demons out of a man (or two) in the region of the Gerasenes (Mk. 5:1-20), and a host of demons out of Mary Magdalene (Lk. 8:2). There is the mention of certain angels being bound to the "abyss"[107]—as Satan will be at the onset of the millennial reign—but these are most definitely not allusions to Gehenna (the place Jesus described as the final location of the wicked). Based on the aforementioned passages involving possession, the case also cannot be made that *all* of the fallen angels even exist in the abyss at present. The point is that, just as it is with Satan, we hear of no demonic activity occurring within the depths of hell.

There is a good reason why the forces of darkness are not associated (in the present tense) with hell in the Bible—hell is not currently a reality for anyone. It was previously noted that hell is the place *prepared* for Satan and his angels. In the same verse, we see that hell is also the destination for those who choose to follow Satan rather than Christ (Mt. 25:41). But the main point remains the most pivotal—Satan and the fallen angels, the very entities that hell is/will be designed for, do not even exist there at the present time. As a

---

[106] See Lorenzi's *Devil's in Art* for good examples of such imagery.

[107] Passages such as Luke 8:31, and Revelation 9:1-2; 20:1 speak of the abyss as being a locale for imprisoned demons. What demons are confined to the abyss is not fully understood, but there can be little doubt that some presently exist there. On the other hand, some demons clearly are not confined to the abyss because they are presently able to affect the comings and goings of our world.

matter of logic, it stands to reason that Satan's deceased followers do not exist in hell right now, either. *At the moment, no one is suffering in hell.*

Within the New Testament, any discussion about the "lake of fire" (Gehenna) or the place of everlasting punishment revolves around the end of this age. The book of Revelation summarizes this point well: "And the devil, who deceived them, was thrown into the lake of burning sulfur, where the beast and the false prophet had been thrown. They will be tormented day and night for ever and ever" (20:10). This exact point in time quite obviously occurs in the context of Christ's return and the ultimate separation of the righteous and the wicked. It appears that even the fallen angels (demons) are well aware that God is going to administer their punishment at a specific point in the future. The Gospel of Matthew (and its synoptic parallels) makes this point clear for us when it tells of Jesus' confrontation with two demon-possessed men:

> "When he arrived at the other side in the region of the Gadarenes, two demon-possessed men coming from the tombs met him. They were so violent that no one could pass that way. 'What do you want with us, Son of God?' they shouted. 'Have you come here to torture us before the appointed time?'"[108]

Clearly, hell is the *future* place of punishment for the forces of evil. If hell is an existence yet to be experienced by Satan (or anyone), what could that potentially reveal to us about the state of the dead? What does this have to do with deceased believers? While the biblical descriptions of hell do not directly tell us something about heaven, they certainly do so indirectly. The question really comes down to this: if the unrepentant do not go directly to Gehenna when they die, then why should we believe that the faithful go directly to heaven when they die?

This notion seems to be deeply flawed from a logical perspective, and is actually in opposition to the overall message of Scripture. It should be noted that a story like Jesus' parable of the Weeds is absolutely incompatible with the perspective that we will go straight to heaven or hell at death.[109]

---

[108] Matthew 8:28-29.

[109] I have mentioned this parable throughout the book. Again, this story is recorded in Matthew 13:24-30 and is explained by Jesus himself in verses 36-43. I *strongly* encourage taking the time to reflect on this story.

If this were true, then the landowner doesn't actually separate the wheat from the weeds when the harvest time comes, as Jesus so clearly revealed. Instead, the story would have to be rewritten, and the landowner (God) would need to tell the servants to separate the weeds (the unrepentant) from the wheat (the righteous) on the spot. If the weeds are not being sent to their everlasting destination during this age, how can the wheat be? They are both supposed to be living together until the harvest, after all. More than that, they are supposed to be completely separated when—and only when—that day comes. As Jesus tells us in his own interpretation of the parable, the harvest is clearly an allusion to the judgment that will occur upon his return (Mt. 13:39).

Now, what does all of this mean to us? Simply put, it means that if believers are entering heaven before the harvest occurs, then Jesus was wrong in his assessment of the judgment and the afterlife. Suffice it to say that this should be a deeply troubling problem for those who think that heaven is the immediate destination for the souls of deceased believers. While heaven and hell are on completely opposite sides of the spectrum, they are inextricably bound in terms of their temporal placement. No one goes to hell immediately after death, and no one instantly goes to live in heaven, either. Again, are we to believe something contrary to what Jesus taught in the parable of the Weeds—that hell is empty, but heaven is full of fallen saints? The entire premise of the ultimate judgment is that all people—whether of the past, present, or future—will be evaluated and justly sent to their appropriate dwelling places at the end of this age. This being the case, it would make very little sense to believe that the souls of deceased human beings are currently occupying either heaven or hell.

WHAT GOD HAS PUT ASUNDER, LET NO MAN JOIN TOGETHER

While the previous section makes a valid point on its own, there are further considerations that stem from it. I previously discussed the conundrum presented within the reality that neither the forces of evil nor the unrepentant currently live in hell. As a matter of logic, deceased believers are not presently living in heaven, either. But certainly, the Bible is clear that there are really only two types of people in this world—those who are going to enjoy the splendors of everlasting life with God, and those who will suffer the torments of Gehenna. I am well aware that the doctrine of *universalism* is now enjoying a resurgence within the church. For those who are not familiar with this belief, it essentially asserts that every person who has ever lived (or will ever live) is ultimately going to be redeemed. Some even believe that Satan will be saved before it's all said and done.

An entire book could (and has by others) be written to refute this belief. For the sake of the nature of this book, it should suffice to say that universalism (or *universal reconciliation*) simply doesn't jive with the overall testimony of the Bible. We have already seen this through evaluating Jesus' parables of The Rich Man and Lazarus and the Weeds, both of which make clear the fact that those who live a godless life will not be saved. There are many, many other parts of Scripture that reflect the same teaching.[110] Among other things, the very existence of hell negates the possibility of universalism. The Bible would never even need to talk about a realm of everlasting torment if it were not actually a possibility that anyone could exist there. Thus, the universalist's quarrel is not with me, but with Jesus and the biblical authors. Putting that issue aside, notice once more that there are three major ways in which the Bible *potentially* describes the interim period:

1) We could immediately depart to heaven or hell as disembodied souls/spirits.
2) We could immediately depart to another intermediate state of existence, like Abraham's bosom or Sheol/Hades, also as disembodied souls/spirits.
3) We could remain in an unconscious state before Christ's coming, as our earthly bodies return to the dust and our souls return to God.

I have already addressed many of the biblical passages that speak to these possibilities, but I now ask you to imagine the logical problems that Christ's teachings about the great judgment present within this discussion. If either of the first two possibilities are correct, how can we actually square those views with the certainty of a "judgment day?"

For anyone who takes Jesus' teachings about heaven and hell seriously, these are sobering facts that should force us to urgently evaluate our own lives. We will either be reckoned among the righteous, or we will be party to the collection of people who have to hear these dreadful words— "depart

---

[110] See Galatians 5:19-21, 2 Thessalonians 1:6-10, 2 Peter 2, and Revelation 22:14-15, just to name a few.

from me, for I never knew you."[111] Of all the issues in life, there are none that even broach the importance of this situation. While the Bible plainly advocates this reality, it is equally unequivocal in its position on *when* this separation will occur. The case I have made throughout this book is that our everlasting destinies will be decided when Christ returns. Though I have touched upon this elsewhere, it may be helpful to add a bit of clarity to this concept. Though the push towards the belief in an ultimate day of judgment began in the Old Testament concept of "the day of the Lord," it was certainly expanded upon as biblical history drew on.[112] The prophet Daniel spoke of a time when the dead would be awakened; "And many of those who sleep in the dust of the earth shall awake, some to everlasting life, and some to shame and everlasting contempt."[113] Notice Daniel's view of the sequence of events at the end—the dead will rise (from their "sleep"), and *then* they will be judged.

During the intertestamental period—the period between what is recorded within the two testaments of the Bible—apocalyptic beliefs continued to form and spread. Among those beliefs were views about the final judgment. The Wisdom of Solomon (or simply *Wisdom*, for short) provides us with a solid sampling of what many within the Jewish community believed about the matter during this time. In Wisdom, God will *later* pronounce judgment on both the righteous and the wicked; the hope of the righteous is "full of immortality," but the wicked will experience only dread when their lawless deeds "convince them to their face."[114] In fact, the wicked will share the same fate as the Devil himself.[115] These are almost certainly allusions to the judgment that we later see so plainly within the New Testament, particularly the destruction of the unrighteous in Revelation 20. Certainly, some of the beliefs that come to us from the intertestamental period align with Daniel's affirmation that our fates will be pronounced at a specified time in the future—judgment day. While both the Old Testament and the works of the intertestamental period certainly suggest the reality of an all-encompassing

---

[111] Matthew 7:23.

[112] In the New Testament, the "Day of the Lord" was certainly understood to be, among other things, the final Day of Judgment. The second coming of Christ was thought to be the central event of this time. For further information about this concept, I refer you to Burge's article, "Day of Christ, God, the Lord," 319-20.

[113] Daniel 12:2.

[114] The Wisdom of Solomon, 3:4 and 4:20.

[115] Ibid. 2:24.

judgment at the climax of human history, the writings of the New Testament undeniably support this belief.

I have already pointed out that when Jesus entered the scene, he affirmed that genuine and complete justice must be viewed in purely eschatological terms. This means that judgment and the separation of the righteous and the wicked are end time matters. As the parable of the Weeds so clearly demonstrates, the righteous and the wicked will be separated for the rest of eternity when the "landowner" returns for the "harvest." Likewise, Paul consistently taught the very same concept, and so does the book of Revelation.[116] The same could be said of every other New Testament text that we may wish to consider, for that matter. Clearly, the future fate of every person on the planet—whether of the past, present, or future—is set to be announced when Christ returns and the great judgment is at hand. In orthodox Christian circles, there are few who would disagree with this point. As sure as this is from a biblical perspective, a philosophical atom bomb rests ominously close to the "afterlife now" crowd.

The problem resides within the following question: if the separation of the righteous and the wicked is placed squarely at the time of Christ's return, then how could such a judgment exist at the present? If we hold to the view that believers are sent to heaven at the moment of death, then judgment has already been pronounced. If we hold to the view that believers are sent to Abraham's bosom, then judgment has also already been pronounced. Likewise, the same applies to the unrepentant if they are vanquished to either Gehenna or Hades. See the problem? Christ's return ceases to be the time that God delivers judgment if every person's fate is decided at the moment of death. Instead, if this view were true, God would actually be making everlasting judgment calls at every step of human existence.

Of course, this presents no problem for those who believe in the immortality of the soul and the TDP. Typically, these beliefs come part and parcel with the concept of *particular judgment*, which promotes the idea that God actually decides the fate of every human being at death. In other words, God decides everyone's ultimate fate at the moment they die, not during

---

[116] Paul discusses this less clearly in a text like Galatians 5:19-26, in which the wicked are said to "not inherit the Kingdom of God." He is much more specific and forceful in 2 Thessalonians 1:5-10, where Paul says that the unrighteous will "suffer the punishment of everlasting destruction." This is almost certainly a reference to Gehenna. Meanwhile, the entire chapter of Revelation 20 (among other parts of the book) makes the ultimate separation of the righteous and the wicked very clear.

the great judgment. This type of individual assessment would certainly be necessary if God is supposed to be determining who should go where during the interim period. The problem is that the Bible says virtually nothing in support of this preliminary hearing.

If the doctrine of particular judgment is correct, then there is not going to be an all-encompassing judgment when Christ returns; there is certainly no *need* for such a thing, at least. Rather, there is a series of smaller judgments that lead to the last. We would first be judged at the moment of death, where we would be sent to one of the places I have mentioned throughout this book (heaven, hell, Hades, etc.) in a disembodied state of being. Then, when Christ returns, we would be judged yet again in order to determine our ultimate destinies. This would lead to either everlasting life with Christ or everlasting condemnation in Gehenna. If we are to suggest the existence of Purgatory, there may yet even be other judgments that evaluate whether we have been properly "purified" or not. Whatever the case, there would be at least *two* major judgments. On this point, I recall the insightful words of William Tyndale when he considered the very same proposition:

> "And ye, in putting them [the departed souls] in heaven, hell, and purgatory, destroy the arguments wherewith Christ and Paul prove the resurrection . . . And again, if the souls be in heaven, tell me why they be not in as good case as the angels be? And then what cause is there of the resurrection?"[117]

For all who have died, and all who will, God is continuously declaring the very things that are supposed to be announced "on the day when God will judge the world."[118] In this view, Christ will return to execute a judgment that has already occurred—literally billions of times, and perhaps multiple times for each person—throughout human history.

The conclusions should be obvious; the judgment aspect of the "day of the Lord" (Joel 1:15), the "day of the Lord Jesus" (2 Cor. 1:14), the "day of Christ" (Phil. 1:10), or whatever we wish to call it, is nothing of the sort. You cannot have an ultimate day of reckoning—which is central to this event—when the dead have already been reckoned. This would be something akin to the expectation of a wedding ceremony—the anticipation builds and builds,

---

[117] William Tyndale, *An Answer to Sir Thomas More's Dialogue*, book four, chapter four, 180-81.
[118] See Acts 17:31.

but when you arrive, you discover that the happy couple eloped six months ago. The ceremony ceases to be the moment when the two were bound in holy matrimony, and is instead merely a chance for others to witness what has been true for quite some time. In the same way that we cannot rightfully call that a "wedding," we cannot pretend that the great judgment is the moment when all of humanity is evaluated and separated. The fate of every human being could either be decided at death or at the return of Christ, but not both.

The belief in a conscious interim period utterly destroys the purpose of the ultimate judgment that the Bible so consistently illustrates. Yet again, we are at a critical point where those who believe in disembodied souls and immaterial afterlives have to make a decision; do they deny the former ideas and accept an unconscious interim period, or do they sacrifice another key biblical principal in order to hold on to their views? Speaking of the belief in immaterial afterlives and ethereal spirit worlds, it is now time to move on to my next point in the greater discussion about the afterlife.

IT'S ALL SUBSTANTIVE

At the end of the previous section, I mentioned that one of the foundational beliefs held within the TDP is that God will sentence all people to one of several possible realms of existence at the moment of death. In essence, this means that each one of us will face our own "particular judgment" immediately after leaving this world, and I have pointed out the fact that there are both biblical and logical problems with this perspective. Now, I turn towards an even deeper problem with this view: a problem that has to do with its underlying assumptions. In order for the doctrine of particular judgment to be true—or for the TDP to be true, for that matter—there must actually be purely immaterial (i.e. non-substantive) realms of existence that can house our immaterial souls during the interim period. A disembodied, immaterial soul requires an immaterial realm.

In this part of the book, I am going to suggest that this belief reveals yet another fundamental misstep in thinking on the part of temporary-disembodiment proponents. More than that, I will suggest that a large number of Christian thinkers—whether of the past or the present—have committed to a number of highly questionable assumptions when it comes to this particular point. Here, I hope to show that it is not possible, in principle, for an immaterial soul to enter into a conscious, disembodied existence after death *because there are no purely immaterial realms to inhabit*. While I realize this may sound like an incredibly bold claim, I feel that it makes the best overall sense of the biblical message.

In the first chapter of the book, I mentioned that Jesus' resurrection body is the best indicator of what our ultimate existence will be like in the new heavens and new earth. Jesus is, after all, the first to be raised from the dead with the perfected type of body that we will all one day be given (1 Cor. 15:20, 49). In this, it is crucial to remember that the resurrected Jesus was not recognized (at least initially) by his appearance, but by his actions and characteristics. Jesus clearly stated that we will not exist as we do now after the resurrection. Rather, we will be "like the angels in heaven" (Mk. 12:25, Mt. 22:30). Jesus could not have intended this statement to pertain only to biological or social issues (like reproduction or marriage) because he was dealing with a group of people (the Sadducees) who were known for rejecting the very premise of the resurrection. The Sadducees were not only wrong because they rejected the belief in the afterlife, but also because their entire understanding of the concept of resurrection was flawed. This is particularly evident in Luke's account of the story, where Jesus specifically mentions that we will be like the angels *because we can no longer die* (20:36). The entire doctrine of the resurrection and the nature of the afterlife are at stake here, not simply issues like childbearing and marriage.

In his writings, Paul further clarified the issue of the angelic body type when he said: "All flesh is not the same flesh, but there is one flesh of men, and another flesh of beasts, and another flesh of birds, and another of fish. There are also heavenly bodies and earthly bodies, but the glory of the heavenly is one, and the glory of the earthly is another" (1 Cor. 15:39-40). Though some have seen the "heavenly bodies and earthly bodies" as relating to the planets, it makes much better sense that Paul was referring to the types of bodies possessed by the angelic beings and the earthly beings.[119] Among others, theologians J.P. Moreland and Scott Rae have suggested that angels

---

[119] The New Testament scholar Leon Morris has summarized the correct view of this passage: "We use this term 'heavenly bodies' as the stars, and some see this as Paul's meaning . . . But this is probably not Paul's thought. He comes to the stars in the next verse, and further, the counterpart of the 'heavenly bodies' in that sense of the term is 'the earth,' not *earthly bodies*. It was an accepted idea that heavenly beings, at least some of them, had bodies." *The First Epistle of Paul to the Corinthians*, 221.

are not truly substantive beings, and that they simply manifest themselves as such when need be.[120]

The problem with this view is that Paul clearly claimed that Jesus' resurrection body is the model for our future bodies, and Jesus confirmed that we will be like the angels after the resurrection. Putting the two together, we can deduce that the angels must also possess bodies that are similar (if not identical in type) to Christ's resurrection body; ". . . as is the heavenly man, so also are those who are of heaven" (1 Cor. 15:48). There is no doubt that the resurrection body will be different than our current bodies in many ways, but both are substantive in some way or another. Besides, if you are only known to manifest yourself in some substantive way then *you are* substantive in nature. If we take the alternative path, we must be prepared to explain just how often something must exist in a physical form in order to be considered physical in nature. The line would be impossible to determine.

Furthermore, it is worth wondering when the angels will be given bodies suitable for living in the new heavens and new earth, *if* they are indeed purely immaterial beings at present. We will need new bodies—and Jesus already possesses one—so it follows that the angels must someday receive bodies, too. That is, if they are going to partake in the same Kingdom that every other being (God included) will share. According to the TDP, this would actually mean that even the angels presently dwell in an undesirable form; as "unembodied beings," they must yearn to be given bodies. Those poor angels. Why would God refuse to give them bodies after all of this time? It seems that immaterial existence is, yet again, found wanting.

At this point, one simply has to ask the question: if immaterial existence is so clearly inferior to substantive existence, why would we subsist in such a way during the interim period, and why would God purposely create the angels as immaterial beings? Setting aside the horrific logical enigma, the previous points would be very difficult to square with Paul's aforementioned statement in 1 Corinthians 15:48, which ensures that the heavenly beings have heavenly bodies. On a final note, the Bible never speaks about angelic beings in any other way than to suggest that they are tangible entities that can be seen, heard, and physically experienced. To say that they are normally immaterial—which can only be taken to mean "material-less," intangible,

---

[120] Moreland and Rae, *Body and Soul*, 24–25.

non-substantive, or any of the like—[121] is to make an argument from silence. We simply have no concrete reason to believe that angels are immaterial beings, and they *never* show up in the Bible as such. As far as we can tell, both Jesus and the angels are substantive beings.

Consider a passage of Scripture that would appear, on the surface, to contradict my claims. The Gospel of Mark records that Jesus cast an entire group of demons (a "legion," as they indicated) out of a man, sending them into a herd of pigs (5:1-20). The very idea that these demons were spoken of in terms of being *within* the man (and pigs) indicates to some that demons must be immaterial, spaceless entities. It is worth noting that many of the church's most prominent philosophers and theologians use identical terminology when attempting to prove the necessity of a transcendent being in the creation of our universe. In fact, some would suggest that viewing God as an unembodied mind comes part and parcel with the basic tenets of "classical theism."[122] But these views are misguided. The fact that Jesus propelled the demons *from* somewhere (the man) *to* somewhere else (the pigs) reveals that demons cannot possibly be completely immaterial, spaceless entities. Something that is immaterial (again, meaning literally "non-material" or having no substance) cannot occupy any space, anywhere. A truly immaterial object or entity could never be said to be "here" or "there" because it could not occupy any single place, point, inertial frame, or anything of the sort, regardless of how one may choose to view the deepest issues of physics (like space and time).[123]

In the same way that one could not move an abstract object (like a number or an idea) from one place to another because it cannot occupy any space, Jesus could not have thrown purely immaterial, spaceless entities (as angels and demons are alleged to be) from one physical location to another.

---

[121] If something else is intended by the word "immaterial," its users may do well to opt for a better term.

[122] In a Q & A session, Dr. William Lane Craig posited that the transcendent cause responsible for creating the universe must be an ". . . uncaused, beginningless, changeless, immaterial, timeless, spaceless, and enormously powerful cause. . .." "Is the Cause of the Universe an Uncaused, Personal Creator of the Universe?"

[123] For those who would like additional perspective on how God (and other heavenly beings) is involved in our understandings of such things as time and space, I highly recommend William Lane Craig's, *Time and Eternity: Exploring God's Relationship to Time*. Here, Craig provides a masterful history of thought on the matter, as well as an honorable contribution to the discussion.

Something that is immaterial, intangible, incorporeal, spaceless, and the like, would necessarily exist everywhere at once without boundary; it could not exist within a man or a herd of swine because both would be spatially confined locations. In fact, it even seems impossible to discuss the nature of things like the heavenly realm or beings like God and the angels without employing the language of substance. When we make basic statements like "the Father in heaven," we are suggesting that God exists in a spatial location; God is in heaven, not everywhere. Jesus "returned" to the Father because the Father was not present on earth. Even God is not immaterial and without spatial boundary, especially given the fact that the Son of God became incarnate (became flesh) in the man Jesus.

For further clarity, consider our church creeds. This is a bit of a complex issue, but I believe it is something that is absolutely worth mentioning. Both the Nicene and Niceno-Constantinopolitan Creeds refer to the "consubstantial" (meaning "shared," essentially) nature of the relationship between the three persons of the Trinity—the Father, the Son, and the Holy Spirit. Both record that Jesus is ". . . of one substance with the Father." The word used here for "substance" originally comes from the Greek *homoousion*, meaning literally "(the) same being," and later from the Latin *ejusdemque substantiae*, meaning "the same substance." While this may only appear to be fancy theological jargon, there is a profound point to be made in light of this terminology. If God is truly immaterial—meaning God is neither spatially extended nor spatially confined—then there cannot be any "substance" to refer to; God would literally exist everywhere, and in everything. In other words, there could be no distinction between God's being and everything else that exists. For all intents and purposes, God would be the universe, and everything within the universe would be part of God. This would mean that the ancient creeds do not affirm the shared divinity of the three persons of the Trinity, but instead affirm the shared divinity of all things with God.

Presumably, this would even be true of God's relationship to Satan and the forces of evil. If God is in everything and is part of everything, then even the Devil is somehow part of God's being. But any serious Christian should understand that this way of thinking belongs to pantheism and the various faiths of eastern mysticism (or Thomism, unfortunately). Good Christian theology holds that God is His own being, existing independent of any created thing, and that God exists as an eternal relationship of three persons. The ways in which we both think and speak about God suggest a being of substantive quality, and this is simply unavoidable. A lot more could be said (and would need to be said) in proving the necessity of substance with regards to God's existence, but we cannot stray too far from the thrust of this entire discussion. Contrary to popular reasoning, Jesus' encounters with demonic forces actually provides evidence of their substantive and spatial condition rather than offering support for the view that they are unembodied, immaterial, and spaceless. As though this were not enough, the substantive nature of the angels is further validated when we consider that the very place the angels dwell (the heavenly realm) is not immaterial in nature, either.

Legitimate Christian scholars never make the case that Jesus did not fully take up human form, or that he only appeared to be substantive. In fact, the apostles battled this very idea when they wrote against the Gnostic Docetists in the first century,[124] and similar heresies were battled throughout the proceeding centuries of the early church. Moreover, it is biblically inaccurate to say that Jesus does not *presently* exist in substantive form, as though he only temporarily possessed his resurrection body. As previously mentioned, other heavenly beings function the same way in that their type of bodily existence allows them to be seen and heard on earth while also enabling them to vanish from our sight (to the heavenly realm). Before thinking this proves the idea that angelic (or demonic) entities are immaterial beings that periodically manifest, recall that Jesus' resurrection body proved otherwise. If a demon temporarily invades our world in order to possess a human being, or an angel appears in an altered physical form, how is that overly different than when Jesus mysteriously strolled through a locked door?[125] For that matter, Jesus seemed to appear in our realm and disappear into the heavenly realm at will.[126] Jesus had a body, and there is no reason to think that other heavenly beings do not.

Jesus did not depart to some location in outer space in between

---

[124] The Docetists believed that Jesus' fleshly appearance was essentially an illusion. Like most of Gnostic thought, this perspective was the product of a very negative view of the physical world, which of course included the human body. Not surprisingly, they borrowed heavily from Platonic thought. Their heresy was probably what spurred the apostle John to write the famous words of 1 John 4:2: "Every spirit that acknowledges that Jesus Christ *has come in the flesh* is from God" (emphasis mine).

[125] These events are recorded in John 20:19-28. Actually, Jesus passes through a locked door on two separate occasions within this passage. The implication is that Jesus walked through the door, not that someone unlocked it for him.

[126] See Luke 24:13-35 for a great example of this type of activity.

resurrection appearances—as the medieval, three-story view of the universe would inaccurately assert—but to a realm that is not spatially bound to our own. Speaking of Jesus, Paul's words in Colossians 1:15-16 read as follows: "He is the image of the invisible God, the firstborn over all creation. For by him all things were created: things in heaven and on earth, visible and invisible, whether thrones or powers or rulers or authorities; all things were created by him and for him." Notice that Paul did not say "physical and immaterial," but "visible and invisible." He even noted that Jesus is the "image of the invisible God," not the "image of the immaterial" God. It is precisely these "invisible" things that characterize the heavenly realm and the beings within it. The fact that we do not always see the forces at work in our world does not necessarily mean that they are immaterial in nature. As Jesus' resurrection appearances (and disappearances) help to illustrate, it is actually unlikely that those from the heavenly realm are anything other than embodied beings.

On this front as well, to suggest that demons must be immaterial entities in order to be capable of possessing human beings is to grossly misunderstand the connection between the earthly and heavenly realms. Interactions between heavenly beings and earthly beings have no correlation to a concept like *distance*. The heavenly beings—like Jesus, Satan, and the angels (fallen or not)—demonstrate the ability to pass seamlessly from realm to realm, or dimension to dimension, in an instant. You could almost imagine the heavenly realm as a sheet or a film that rests upon our realm of existence. The heavenly beings pass easily between the two realms, without having to travel across the universe or something of the sort. All of this is to say that neither demonic possession nor angelic intervention require that heavenly beings be immaterial, as is typically understood when a demon "invades" a human being. Rather, in a peculiar (yet biblically accurate) way, a heavenly being can exist both within their respective realm and the earthly realm at once.

Put another way, heavenly beings can have an effect on earthly beings without "leaving" their respective realm, and so they need not be immaterial at all. In this sense, events or entities that appear to us to be immaterial only seem that way because we are not capable of entering into the heavenly realm. Hence, we are not able to be completely aware of what all may be occurring because of our human limitations. I think this is precisely the situation we read about in 2 Kings 6:17, when Elisha's servant was concerned because they were surrounded by Aramean soldiers; "And Elisha prayed, 'open his eyes LORD, so that he may see.' The LORD opened the servant's eyes, and he looked and saw the hills full of horses and chariots of fire all around Elisha." Heaven's army was with them the entire time, but the servant could not see it. It is not that they were *immaterial,* but that they were *invisible* to the human eye: concealed in the heavenly realm. There is probably a lot going on around us all of the time that we are only vaguely (if at all) aware of. Personally, I find this to be a very intriguing prospect. To think: a hidden world that is occurring right alongside of our own!

Something like demonic possession—such as the aforementioned demonic swine story—should not be understood as an event in which an immaterial being houses itself within a substantive being, but as an event where a substantive being from another realm *obtains control over* someone in the earthly realm. This is no doubt what Paul had in mind when he said, "For our struggle is not against flesh and blood, but against the rulers, against the authorities, against the powers of this dark world and against *the spiritual forces of evil in the heavenly realms*" (Eph. 6:12, emphasis mine). Possession can occur in this manner because there is no spatial distance between the two realms, and heavenly beings are capable (biblically speaking) of passing in and out of our realm at will. If we possessed both the identical substance and power of the heavenly beings, we too could probably pass between these realms. But that is one of the key differences between the "natural body" and the "spiritual body." Perhaps that is why Paul was so emphatic that we will need new bodies in order to live in God's Kingdom. *New* bodies, not *no* bodies.

While Jesus' resurrection appearances proved that we must reimagine the nature of the resurrection *soma* (body), there can be no doubt that he still possessed (and possesses) one. A bodiless resurrection is not a "resurrection" at all. In many respects, this is the miracle of the Incarnation—the Son of God was willing to bind himself to humanity by becoming one us. After laying down his life, he solidified this union into eternity by receiving the first of the resurrection bodies. He became what we will someday be. If Jesus simply disposed of the resurrection body after the Ascension, then his union with humanity was merely temporary. A similar type of existence can also be attributed to the angelic beings, though they are also quite different from us and are capable of manifesting in ways we cannot fully imagine.[127]

---

[127] See Joe's story in the section, "Other Entities." There, I discuss the possibility that angels can perhaps even manifest themselves in human likeness. This does not mean that they don't possess their own unique bodies. Instead, such an event simply proves the lack of limitations associated with the angelic form.

As this section heads toward a close, we must now ask what all of this can really tell us about the nature of heaven. In both Jewish and Christian history, "heaven" has often been considered to be an ethereal, otherworldly place that existed somewhere in the sky. While some of us today understand—just as Jesus and some of the biblical authors understood—that heaven is not some place contained within our physical universe, even trained theologians still tend to view it as a purely spiritual realm. By "spiritual," we are asked to think of something immaterial and non-substantive. But, as I said at the onset of this chapter: *is* heaven an immaterial place? Do we have any biblical basis for believing that it is not?

As I have said throughout this book and discussed in this chapter, heaven is most properly understood as a realm of existence. Among other things, Jesus' resurrection appearances tell us something about heaven. The period of time in which Jesus showed himself and interacted with his followers after the Resurrection—which some have called the "lost forty days"—reveals that heaven and earth are not so much *spatially* separated as they are *dimensionally* separated. Whenever Jesus would appear to his followers and then abruptly vanish, he was not slipping in and out of a body, as though he sometimes existed as a naked spirit. Further, Jesus was not flying off to space and returning in some cranked-up rocket ship. Rather, he was passing—body and all—between the earthly realm and the heavenly realm. This is probably the best explanation of what angels (and demons) do whenever they interact with our realm as well.

Though much of the story appears to be parabolic in nature, the book of Job describes Satan (a fallen angel) as being a member of the royal court who spends most of his time roaming the earth. Jesus told us that Satan was thrown to the earth, meaning he fell from constant enjoyment with God within the heavenly realm to a lesser state of being within both that realm and ours. Jesus did not intend us to believe that Satan was literally tossed "down" from space. Satan is present in our realm, but the story of Job shows us that he is still capable of venturing into the heavenly realm (he reports to God, Job 1:6-7). Even if we do not glean a literal account of Satan from the book of Job in any way, we still have the apostle Paul referring to Satan as "the ruler of the kingdom of the air" (Eph. 2:2), which is clearly a name alluding to his involvement in the heavenly court. At the same time, Jesus called Satan the "prince of this world" (Jn. 14:30), which shows his strong connection with our earthly affairs. To some degree, it appears that Satan has ties to both realms.

These examples are not the only places where we see heaven and earth overlap. The Garden of Eden represents life in a pre-Fall world: a world in which the heavenly realm intersected with our own in such a way that there was little to no separation between them. Essentially, heaven and earth were one. This is evidenced by the fact that God walked through the same garden inhabited by Adam and Eve (Gen. 3:8).[128] Most intentionally, it is this type of existence that the Bible concludes with in the book of Revelation. There is a new heaven and a new earth, and they intersect naturally together once more. Rather than talking about traveling to an ethereal spirit world, this is what we ought to be envisioning when we refer to "dying and going to heaven." In that Kingdom, there will be no death, no sickness, no estrangement from God, and no dimensional separation between heaven and earth. God once again walks with us "in the cool of the day," as our realms completely merge for the rest of eternity.

Perhaps the mistake that most theologians and religious thinkers have made is to assume that our existence is the only place where physical life is the norm: that immaterial existence is the default. What exactly has made us believe that God intended our world to be the anomaly? Are we to believe that an immaterial being (God) created a bunch of immaterial beings (angels) to inhabit a purely immaterial realm (heaven), but then decided to create material beings (us) to live in a separate, but undeniably material realm of existence (earth)? Though every other being in existence is supposedly immaterial and lives in an immaterial realm, we were created to be material beings who live in a material world. While our existence is entirely substantive, nothing else is. Ask yourself: does that make any sense at all? But there is even more to this. God's ultimate act of redemption, and the central element of his union with humanity, was to cause the Son to become a fully embodied human being, and to later give him the first of the resurrection bodies. At the end of the age, God's plan for his entire creation is to make a new heaven and a new earth; both of which will be *substantive*, not immaterial, realities.

It should be noted that in order for Christ to have taken the perfected human form back with him to the heavenly realm, the heavenly realm must indeed be the type of place where substantive beings live. Imagine the absurdity of an embodied, resurrected Jesus floating about amongst a bunch

---

[128] Even if this verse is taken figuratively, it would still illustrate the fact that the union between God and humanity—and between the earthly and heavenly realms—was in its intended, unbroken condition.

of immaterial beings in an ether world. While it would perhaps be possible for Christ to be the sole example of tangible existence within the entire heavenly realm, it simply makes much better sense to believe that the entire realm is similarly substantive (in whatever way that may be). So, the question I'm really getting at is this: why did God create *substantive* beings to inhabit a *substantive* world, and promise to make an all new *substantive* existence where everyone—humanity, the angels, and even He—would live for the rest of eternity, when the realm that both He and the angels presently occupy is immaterial?

The only logical conclusion is that material existence is far more than a temporary or optional state of being. God created physical beings for a reason, and the purpose can hardly be to allow our immaterial souls to express themselves in material ways. But whenever the human soul is considered to be more essential than the body, or is regarded as a being that can consciously exist by itself, the physical world is made into just that—a disposable canvas on which the soul temporarily paints its mural. This cannot be so. If the soul can consciously exist by itself, then our physical bodies (and all of physical existence, for that matter) are unnecessary. Bodies are added ingredients to a recipe that doesn't call for them. I will most definitely return to this point later in the chapter.

Though seen within a spectrum of variation, bodily existence is described as being essential to all of God's created beings. God is a spiritual being. The Scriptures tell us as much.[129] However, I do not believe that being "spiritual" is equivalent to being "immaterial," for all of the reasons I have mentioned. But even if God—yes, the sole being of eternality and infinity—once existed in immaterial form, there can be little doubt that He is now connected to embodied existence. Ever since the resurrection of Jesus, God always will be. If we take God's union with humanity seriously, then this is the ultimate result of Jesus' death, resurrection, and ascension.

It appears, then, that substantive existence is the only genuine mode of existence. This is how everything operates. This is God's design for all things. God made man in His image. Why shouldn't we view substantive existence as a characteristic of that image? Though different from our own bodies (and much improved), both Jesus and the angels possess the "spiritual body"

---

[129] See Genesis 1:2 and John 4:24, for examples of this fact. This makes the Incarnation and Jesus' reception of the resurrection body all the more crucial because they are evidence of God binding Himself to our realm of existence. Even God exists, however strange it may be to say, in bodily form.

within the heavenly realm, which is also somehow substantive in nature. That is how important bodily existence is in God's plans for His creation. None of God's created beings exist in a purely immaterial way, nor does He. Likewise, no past, present, or future realm of existence can be described in such a way, either. All of this explains exactly why I find the idea that our souls will temporarily live in an immaterial realm during the interim period to be so incredibly irrational. Still, there are even more reasons why I feel this way. As I hope to continue to demonstrate, the TDP simply fails to uphold the centrality of the body in God's created order.

JUST ADD BODY

As difficult as it is to square the biblical certainty of a judgment day with the doctrine of particular judgment, and as questionable as it is to assert that purely immaterial realms even exist to begin with, there are yet other difficult issues for temporary-disembodiment advocates to reconcile. Yes, there are more powerful reasons to reject the idea that the soul will consciously survive the death of the body: that we will "die and go to heaven," or anything of the sort. The next two sections of the book present what are probably (in my opinion) the most powerful arguments in favor of my view, which is why I have saved them until now. These are the arguments that also present the most tremendous difficulties to the TDP, and to any perspective that views the soul as being capable of conscious existence apart from the body. I'll spare you (the reader) any more build up, and will cut to the chase. Simply put, our ability to live as disembodied spirits would render the point of a resurrection body utterly meaningless.

Throughout history, the belief that God sentences human beings to either heaven or hell (via particular judgment) at the moment of death has been the official view of the Catholic Church,[130] and probably the most popular view within the Protestant churches. The belief that people are judged and sentenced to another intermediate realm, like Abraham's bosom or Hades, has also seen relative popularity. Though the immediate destinations may be different, it is fair to say that either God's everlasting Kingdom or Gehenna's everlasting torment is the final result of both views. Similarly, both views assert that God judges the dead on at least two different occasions. Neither of these elements are the most significant commonalities between these

---

[130] "Catechism of the Catholic Church." Online version, pp. 266-267.

perspectives though. More essential is the basic assumption that our "souls," "spirits," or what have you, are actually able to consciously exist during the time between our deaths and our resurrections.

Throughout this book, I have made the case that such an idea is neither biblically nor logically sound, and that it owes more to Greek philosophy than it does to scriptural testimony. It is just as Dinesh D'Souza, co-founder of the Y God Institute and former president of Kings College, said concerning this particular belief: "Oddly enough, this idea was first articulated not in biblical or Quaranic sources, but rather in Greek philosophy."[131] I have spent the vast majority of the book attempting to prove this very point—that belief in a disembodied interim period or afterlife is grounded in Greek philosophy rather than biblical teaching—based on the biblical texts themselves. While it is very important whether or not one agrees with my textual interpretations and logical explanations to this point, it is actually irrelevant with regards to the case I am making in this particular section. The arguments within this portion of the book would stand even if the others did not. For this reason, I will lump together all of the views that support a conscious, disembodied existence and scrutinize them with the same argument. Whether we are talking about heaven, hell, Abraham's bosom, Hades, Purgatory, or any view in between, they all share the common belief that we will dwell in an interim existence without a body. It is this point, I believe, that displays the greatest conundrum of all.

While I have spent a great deal of time explaining the principles of death, there is one point that is specifically important to re-establish—death is the absence of life. If the biblical writers intended us to believe that death merely represents an immediate transition from one type of life to another, then why invoke the word to begin with? Why not simply refer to the various *transitions of life*? If this were the case, "death" would scarcely be the immense tragedy that the biblical authors made it out to be, and we understand it to be. In all reality, Genesis 3:19 describes death as being the ultimate result of sin. Paul reaffirmed this when he said, "the wages of sin is death" (Rom. 6:23), as though death is the end point for that which is opposed to God. In perhaps the most telling remark in all of Scripture concerning the horror of death, Paul described death as the "final enemy to destroyed" (1 Cor. 15:26). Notice the fact that Paul felt as though death had not yet been entirely destroyed, even though Christ had been raised from the dead. Instead, death's power

---

[131] Dinesh D'Souza, *Life After Death*, 42.

will finally be shattered when it does not exist anymore. Christ became the first to conquer death *and* be given the new body, but death will not "lose its sting" until all of his followers do the same.

The point is that death is a problem: a very big problem. Death marks the cessation of life, not more life. If it were not so, then the term need not exist in the first place. This reality is clearly illustrated by the very concept of resurrection, which means to be "raised back" to life. Specifically, resurrection is a physical (bodily) occurrence and not an immaterial one. The book of Revelation makes this clear in discussing the millennial glory of those who had been martyred for their faith: "They came to life and reigned with Christ a thousand years" (20:4). The phrase "came to life" (*ezēsan*)—as the NASB correctly translates it—displays my point, since one cannot "come to life" if he or she is already somehow living. Amazingly, more "traditional" views often fail to make this distinction. Instead, they diminish the horrific nature of death to the realm of relative unimportance. Unfortunately, a sizeable number of Christian scholars—of both the past and the present— would vehemently disagree with this take on the issue. But this is just one of the problems that must be addressed.

Two of the critical aspects concerning most concepts of body-soul dualism are that the human soul is viewed as being superior to the body, and that it is thought to be immortal by nature.[132] This was apparently the view that showed up in the church at Corinth, and it had much in common with Gnostic philosophy/theology. Though the roots of this belief significantly predate the early church, the church certainly added justification for this view in later centuries. D'Souza describes the role that popular medieval Christianity played concerning the issues of the soul and the afterlife:

> "The Middle Ages had a three-story view of the universe,
> with heaven up in the sky, earth in the middle, and hell
> down below. With the collapse of the Ptolemaic universe
> and the rise of Newtonian astronomy, it became increasingly
> difficult to specify the physical locations of heaven and

---

[132] Axiological dualism, for example, essentially asserts that the body and the soul, though both equally real, are not equal in value. True to most philosophical conceptions of body-soul dualism, axiological dualists almost always end up marginalizing the importance of the physical world and the body. This is precisely the sort of thinking we also see in Platonic dualism and most of the Gnostic understandings on the matter.

hell. Newtonian physics also included laws of matter that seemed difficult to square with the notion that bodies can somehow survive past death or be permanently restored. Many Christians began to rethink their ideas of the soul, heaven, and hell. The Platonic idea of the immortality of the soul became newly attractive because it avoided the cosmological difficulty. If what survives us is only the immaterial soul, then there is no need to explain how our bodies survive our deaths."[133]

Mark this as the second major reason for affirming the immortality of the soul—which inherently views the soul as being superior to the body— that has absolutely nothing to do with the Bible. It is on this point, in particular, that I find inconsistencies within many of the views offered by church theologians, both of the past and the present. By "inconsistent," I do not mean that theologians often differ with one another as to whether or not this view is promoted within the biblical texts; *on the surface*, most try to denounce the idea that the soul is superior to the body. Rather, I mean that their conclusions often differ with their interpretive efforts.

Ages ago, the esteemed church historian Tertullian illustrated this point well in his writings. On one such occasion, he recorded the following:

> "When the resurrection of the saints is completed, the destruction of the world and the conflagration of judgment will be effected; we shall be 'changed in a moment' into the angelic substance, by the putting on of incorruption (1 Corinthians 15:52-3), and we shall be transferred to the heavenly kingdom."[134]

While Tertullian was correct in his view that believers will be changed into the "angelic substance" at the resurrection, there are problems with other parts of this statement. Based on this view of the afterlife, one would assume that Tertullian's position revolved entirely around the great judgment and the "putting on of incorruption" at the resurrection; he directly says as much, after all. Strangely, he ends up adopting the belief that both judgment and

---

[133] Dinesh D'Souza, *Life After Death*, 47.
[134] Tertullian, *Adversus Marcionem*, III.xxiv. 3-6, 246-8.

immaterial existence *precede* the final state of believers. When elsewhere writing about the judgment and the afterlife, he directly references "paradise" as a "place of divine delight appointed to receive the spirits of the saints."[135]

As I have previously mentioned, some rabbinic traditions viewed paradise as the place of bliss that man had lost through the Fall. Over time, it came to be viewed by some as the place for fallen saints.[136] As we saw in both the story of the criminal on the cross (Lk. 23:32-43) and Revelation 2:7, the biblical view of "paradise" is—except for Paul's use of the term as the "third heaven" (2 Cor. 12:1-4)—an affirmation of the hope in the fulfillment of God's Kingdom.[137] To at least a certain extent, Tertullian displayed the tendency to place our everlasting destinies squarely in the context of the end of the age while spuriously tossing out a contradictory view. I would add that the very language of this view seems to be rooted in the parable of the Rich Man and Lazarus, which was already shown to be a rather tenuous piece of evidence for the TDP. While Tertullian's perspective serves as evidence from antiquity about the aforementioned "inconsistency" issues, modern scholarship may actually prove the point to a greater extent.

Take imminent philosopher and theologian William Lane Craig's view of the matter, for example. At first, Craig makes a fantastic case against the absurdity that the soul is superior to the body:

> "The first and most fundamental truth that we must hold on to is that the biblical hope of immortality is physical, bodily resurrection. I repeat: The biblical hope for immortality is physical, bodily resurrection. The biblical hope is not that the soul will someday be separated from the body and fly off to heaven and be forever with God in heaven in this disembodied existence."[138]

All of this is correct. As you may have noticed, this is the very case I have been making throughout the book. But for whatever reason, Craig does not continue on with this line of thinking. When we reach the pivotal point where the interim period comes into question, his story shifts rather abruptly; "In between your death and your resurrection you will exist as a disembodied

---

[135] See *The Christian Theology Reader,* 614.

[136] H.A. Kent Jr., "Paradise," 891.

[137] Refer back to chapter two's section, "Prowlers in Paradise," to review this case.

[138] William L. Craig, "What Happens When We Die?"

soul, a soul without a body, in a conscious state."[139] This notion almost completely contradicts his prior statement. While the thought of existing as a disembodied soul for the rest of eternity is absurd to Craig, it is a completely acceptable mode of existence during the interim period, however long that may actually be. While you are trying to grasp how Craig's two views could possibly mesh, let's have a look at another perspective on the matter.

Ben Witherington III has also demolished some of these false notions about the soul throughout his many theological writings. In one such instance, he says:

> "The term *psuche* in the New Testament really shouldn't be translated as 'soul,' as it usually refers to our natural life breath . . . this has nothing to do with some nonmaterial part of a human that Greeks called the soul. It has to do with simply being alive with natural life breath in us."[140]

To Witherington, the *psuche* is not "you" as a conscious being, but is a component of "you." It is a necessary quality of what constitutes a human being, not some separate being living within a body. As he accurately points out, that was a belief held by many Greeks of that day. This is all the more reason why his later remarks are so curious. When dealing with the time between death and the resurrection, Witherington changes his tune to that of Craig's. In the very same section quoted above, he goes on to say that both 2 Corinthians 5 and the parable of the Rich Man and Lazarus illustrate that ". . . the naked spirit of a person goes on to be with the Lord." He further claims that the book of Revelation ". . . makes equally clear that when Christians die they do go to be with the Lord; they do go to heaven."[141]

Here, we have another fervent effort to separate the orthodox Christian perspective of the body-soul relationship from the normative pagan, Platonic, or Gnostic understandings of the matter. Unfortunately, the attempt actually ends up bringing all of these views into alignment. If the soul consciously survives death—it can essentially be "you" without the need of a body—then the soul is the element of human existence that matters most. The body is clearly subordinate to the soul.

For the sake of proving the point, consider just one more example.

---

[139] Ibid.
[140] Ben Witherington III, *Revelation and the End Times*, 65.
[141] Ibid. 65-66.

This text comes from another of the elite biblical scholars of our time, N.T. Wright. Wright is one of the church's foremost defenders of the true Christian teachings about the resurrection of Jesus and our magnificent hope in the afterlife. Throughout his book, *Surprised by Hope*, he is absolutely emphatic that the ultimate hope for believers is *not* to live in heaven as disembodied spirits for the rest of eternity, and that the reception of new physical bodies that are fit to live in a renewed creation is actually the objective: or as Wright so often puts it, the goal is "life *after* life after death." To these points, I truly say *amen*. But then, just as the others we have previously evaluated, Wright makes an astonishing compromise when the issue of the interim period arises. Perhaps the clearest example of this is when he is discussing a notion that we have already covered: that the sleep-death analogy refers only to the body and not to the soul. It is on this topic that he says, ". . . sleep here means that the body is 'asleep' in the sense of 'dead,' while the *real person*—however we want to describe him or her—continues."[142]

This is at least a bit mystifying. For Wright, the necessity of the physical body—both in this life and the next—is at the very center of Jesus' resurrection and the entire hope of the Christian faith. But when asked what happens immediately after death, his answer is that our souls continue right on without a body to join them. Moreover, the use of the phrase "the real person" clearly suggests that the soul is the element of human existence that matters most; the soul is the "real us," and the body ultimately has little to do with what constitutes the "real us." To that, all who have Gnostic and/or Platonic leanings say *amen*.

However, it would be unfair to stop there. While admissions like these are rather difficult to explain, Wright's overall perspective seems to be extremely close to my own. When interviewed by *Time Magazine*, he was recorded as describing what the intermediate state is like; "We know that we will be with God and with Christ, resting and being refreshed. Paul writes that it will be conscious, but compared with being bodily alive, it will be like being asleep."[143] Notice that he previously said it is only the body that "sleeps," and not the soul. This contradiction aside, it's difficult to tell what to make of this. On the one hand, we are conscious. On the other hand, our interim existence is essentially like a sleep-state. If we are talking about a state of existence that

---

[142] N.T. Wright, *Surprised by Hope*, 171 (emphasis mine).

[143] See David Biema's article in *Time Magazine*, entitled, "Christians Wrong About Heaven, Says Bishop."

is, for all intents and purposes, not conscious in the sense that we *currently* understand consciousness, then we may well be saying the same thing.

If this is an accurate assessment of his position, then Wright is not truly in alignment with scholars like William Lane Craig, J.P. Moreland, Gary Habermas, or any other TDP supporter, in any appreciable way because many of the examples used to support this position describe a state of being that is thoroughly *conscious* in nature.[144] Furthermore, the typical believer certainly doesn't think that we depart to heaven in order to exist in a virtually unconscious state of being. Rather, most people who talk about "dying and going to heaven" believe that an immediate departure to be with God would result in a drastically heightened sense of awareness and a much more enjoyable existence. It would seem, then, that Wright's general perspective is actually closer to that of theologians like Tyndale, Wycliffe, Luther, and others (myself included), than it is to the "traditional" Christian view (the TDP) of the interim period. I hope that is the case.

The previous views offer some interesting questions. If the union of the body and the soul is what causes us to be living beings, how can the soul consciously survive—independent of the body—after we die? Put another way, how can it be required that the soul exists with its physical counterpart (the body) in order for us to be functioning (alive) human beings, when the soul is essentially a being of its own? The takeaway from the previous perspectives is that there is a tendency, even among scholars who are largely on point, to run into problems when explaining the logistics of the TDP. While they uphold the true biblical teachings about the essential unity of the body and soul, they mysteriously disregard these principles when it comes to a discussion about the state of the dead. It seems as though many scholars want it both ways. On the one hand, they know that affirming the need for a body is absolutely critical, given the undeniable biblical evidence on the matter. On the other hand, they feel bound to affirm a disembodied existence between death and the resurrection.

In order to uphold both views, they are simply willing to go through a

---

[144] Texts like the parable of the Rich Man and Lazarus (Lk. 16:19-31), Hebrews 12:23, and Revelation 6:9-11, are all frequently used as evidence in favor of the TDP. The problem is that these passages, and others used to support the position, most definitely describe the interim period as being a conscious one (if taken literally, which you would need to do). This involves people talking back and forth, thinking through issues, and crying out to God for justice. These are hardly things that would qualify as a drastically lessened sense of consciousness, much less a sleep-state.

laborious theological balancing act. Theologian Adam Kotsko has made this very same observation, summarizing it with incredible accuracy:

> "Attempts to reconcile belief in the resurrection with belief in the immortality of the soul has generated considerable intellectual gymnastics. This perhaps indicates that the two doctrines are not a natural fit, and indeed many contemporary theologians of a more traditional bent have significantly de-emphasized the immortality of the soul in favor of the resurrection."[145]

Though many of these "contemporary theologians" (some of which were previously referenced) have indeed begun to divert attention away from the immortality of the soul and towards the resurrection, the immortality of the soul has by no means vanished from their theological perspectives. Thus, the intellectual gymnastics continue. I will get back to this point towards the end of the chapter, when I discuss my own views in more detail.

In fairness, the overall case that they (and others) are making is that a resurrection body is the *ultimate* hope. While we may live as disembodied spirits during the interim period, bodily existence is the final (and preferred) mode of existence. As it turns out, this idea may prove to be the biggest problem of all within the TDP. Though I do not entirely understand why they would contradict their overall viewpoints in such a way, I cannot help but feel that the reasons are more emotional than evidential; they *want* our souls to consciously depart to heaven when we die, and so do those who read their works. I believe this based on the strength of their efforts in nearly all other theological areas. These are very intelligent people. With that being said, I must believe there are other reasons for their views on this subject. While it would be unacceptable within the fields of biblical and theological studies to support the Gnostic or Platonic concepts of the body-soul relationship, it would apparently be equally egregious to support something like what I am proposing in this book. The result of attempting to "split the difference" is an incoherent hybrid that begs far more questions than it answers.

This is an appropriate time to pull one of the Bible's most important sections about the resurrection back into the fold. In 1 Corinthians 15,

---

[145] Adam Kotsko, "The Resurrection of the Dead: A Religionless Interpretation."

Paul felt compelled to answer the Platonic and Gnostic (at least proto-Gnostic) objections that the human body is a hindrance to our true spiritual nature—that it is somehow an unnecessary evil that will not mark our ultimate existence in the afterlife. He provided an answer to this absurdity by emphasizing the fact that our mortal bodies are fully intended by God, which should have been obvious in the creation account alone. More than that, Paul went so far as to say that physical, bodily existence is completely necessary. It is *necessary*, not evil. It is *necessary*, not unintended. *It is necessary, not optional.* Paul said this quite well in 15:50, 53: "I tell you this, brothers: flesh and blood cannot inherit the kingdom of God, nor does the perishable inherit the imperishable . . . For the perishable must clothe itself with the imperishable, and the mortal with immortality." In order to exist in the world that is to come (the new heavens and new earth), we must have the appropriate physical makeup. We must have the "spiritual body" that Jesus now possesses.

Throughout the entire chapter, Paul never once even hinted that we could live without bodies. In other words, Paul's battle in 1 Corinthians 15 was not against the view that people often think. Though many believe that he was simply fighting for the idea that we will *ultimately* be given new bodies, I don't think that was the case. Rather, Paul was fighting against the idea that we can consciously exist without them: that we could *ever* exist without bodies. We must remember that, according to both Paul and Jesus, even the angels have some type of substantive existence.[146] Paul's issues with the church at Corinth were not only about the future, but about the present as well.

If one believes that we are able to exist in a disembodied state of being—in any way, shape, form, or time—then they would essentially have to agree with the Gnostic and Platonic misconceptions about the nature of the body-soul relationship. They would have to admit that, on their view, the body simply isn't as important as the soul. Consequently, they would also be in disagreement with the apostle Paul on the matter. But the most devastating and essential point within all of this still remains ahead of us. If the body is simply an addition to an already thriving soul, an even deeper question must be raised—why do we need new bodies at all?

---

[146] See Mark 12:25 and its synoptic parallels (Mt. 22:30 and Lk. 20:35-36), as well as 1 Corinthians 15:40.

WHY ADD BODY?

When God created Adam, He did so by breathing life into a body that was formed from the dust of the earth. Physical matter was animated by God's life-giving power in order to produce a living being. This is how Adam was created (Gen. 2:7). In this alone, it is clear that bodies are not simply important items, but are actually essential ones. *Perhaps* God could have made human beings to exist only in immaterial ways—but He didn't. Life in this world, even before the Fall, is dependent upon physical existence. This was precisely Paul's point against his Corinthian opponents. The same logic applies to the next "age" in Paul's statement in 1 Corinthians 15:50, and throughout all of chapter 15, for that matter. If we do not believe that death marks the cessation of conscious existence, then we must believe that the soul consciously survives on its own. This means that wherever the dead consciously dwell—in heaven, hell, Abraham's bosom, Hades, Purgatory, or anywhere else—they are doing so without the need for a physical counterpart. If this is true, the logical conclusions are unavoidable—we do not actually *require* physical bodies in the afterlife.

If we are able to live a comfortable, disembodied life next to father Abraham or even Jesus, then it is difficult to discern why the resurrection body would be essential (or even necessary) in any of this. In either scenario, it seems as though the soul would be doing perfectly fine on its own. Why, then, does God insist on clothing the soul with a body that it doesn't actually require? Theologian James Turner has succinctly summarized this problem, saying, ". . . bodily resurrection would be, at best, metaphysically superfluous for afterlife—i.e. unnecessary for post-mortem existence . . . The Intermediate State renders the eschatological resurrection qualitatively and metaphysically superfluous . . . bodily resurrection is not *necessary* for post-mortem life . . .."[147] This assessment is as devastating to the TDP as it is logically undeniable. Having both read a great deal of literature about this subject and spent countless hours pondering the existential realities of death, I simply haven't seen a satisfying solution to this dilemma.

One might suggest that we didn't *need* the bodies we have now, either. But this is a non-starter, as it ultimately becomes guilty of committing an infinite regress fallacy; why does God need to do anything that He does? Besides, the notion that we didn't need bodies to begin with would actually strengthen

---

[147] James T. Turner, Jr., "We Look for the Resurrection of the Dead," 53-54, 265.

my point. God would unnecessarily be giving us bodies on two different occasions rather than only one. Clearly, we need a body and a soul in order to be mortal human beings because no one can survive without both. The God-given mode of existence in this world is that it takes both components—a body and a soul—in order to be a living person. But to those who believe that our immaterial component consciously proceeds without the body at death, this mode of existence must change entirely. After death, we would suddenly be able to "break the mold," so to speak. Yet, the need for a body at a later date (the resurrection) is added on as an essential requirement for everlasting life. Simply put, the afterlife "being" does not require a body . . . until it receives one.

In this sense, human beings can be compared to computers. In order to get a fully functioning computer, we must have both the external hardware and the internal software. Sure, a keyboard can exist without any software, but what good would it do us by itself? The same could be said of the software components. Without the external hardware components of the computer—the monitor, keyboard, tower, mouse, etc.—the software simply cannot work. To pull an example from science, this situation is eerily reminiscent of the one described by Michael Behe in his famous attack on Darwin's theory of evolution, entitled *Darwin's Black Box*. Among Behe's many arguments for "irreducible complexity" is the example of the mouse trap. His argument is both logical and straightforward. If we were to take away the wooden base, or the hammer, or the spring, or the holding bar from your standard mouse trap, then the whole structure would cease to function in its intended way (as a mouse trap). Since no part can be removed without destroying the entire system, it is irreducibly complex.[148]

The same type of argument can actually be used here to describe the nature of humanity; if either the body or the soul were to be removed, the *being* ceases to function. "You" would cease to be "you" either way. The body and the soul are completely interdependent. The body returns to the ground and the soul returns to God, but neither can function as a living being without the other. When one suggests that our souls can consciously live apart from our bodies, they may as well be saying that a computer file can run itself. This is exactly why it is appropriate to talk about our bodies as "hardware" and our souls as "software."

---

[148] See Behe's, *Darwin's Black Box*, pages 39-48 for a more in-depth look at the concept of "irreducible complexity."

In their co-authored book, *Body and Soul: Human Nature and the Crisis in Ethics*, Moreland and Rae make my case, even though they would actually disagree with my conclusions on the matter. After discussing several of the Old Testament passages that deal with the nature of the afterlife, they reach the following conclusion:

> ". . . it seems apparent that the most natural interpretation is to see the soul-spirit as the locus of personal identity that survives death in a less than fully desirable state and to which a resurrection body will some day be added."[149]

"Less than fully desirable state?" "Will some day be added?" While I largely agree that the soul is the "locus of personal identity"—it is our identity information—I completely reject the notion that we live in a "less than desirable state" as disembodied spirits before the resurrection, or that the new body is essentially just the cherry on top of the soul sundae. This is *exactly* the sort of sentiment for which I wrote this section, and the view that the body is somehow subordinate to the soul is just what Paul denounced in his writings to the church at Corinth.

Furthermore, the view of a disembodied interim period, according to its very supporters, is not overly attractive. Moreland, this time with scholar Gary Habermas, tells us about this sort of existence. While pondering the type of bliss we might enjoy during the interim period, they add the following disclaimer (of sorts):

> "It's hard to speculate on how rich this sort of life will be, but on the face of it, it would seem less desirable than life that includes full-blown sensory experiences normally produced by the body interacting with physical surroundings."[150]

When I read this description, I cannot help but wonder why anyone would even attempt to uphold this position (the TDP). Besides the fact that this particular view is largely devoid of scriptural backing and is almost purely speculation (as they essentially admit), the irony of this position comes to the forefront. Though they mention elsewhere that disembodied life will be

---

[149] Moreland and Rae, *Body & Soul*, 32.
[150] Moreland and Habermas, *Beyond Death*, 232.

"preferable to life here on earth,"[151] they turn around and tell us that it in fact will not be preferable at all. Though we presently enjoy the type of existence mentioned above—a life with "full-blown sensory experiences"—we are supposed to believe that the intermediate state will be an upgrade without those faculties. Which is it?

Furthermore, this is a very different picture of a conscious intermediate state than most believers would ever talk about. This particular view of intermediate disembodiment is leagues away from the standard belief in "dying and going to heaven," and it certainly doesn't resemble the type of existence that a literal view of something like the parable of the Rich Man and Lazarus would suggest. This is especially problematic because these types of passages are supposed to serve as some of the best evidence in favor of their views! If Lazarus, Abraham, and the rich man are all alertly communicating with one another as disembodied spirits—and we are taking this story literally—then we would also have to hold that we can do the same during the interim period. But that's just if we are trying to be consistent in all of this.

It seems that this perspective is not only lacking in biblical support, but is also indicative of the fact that the TDP is not a single "position" at all; after asserting that the interim period is a conscious one, there does not seem to be a consensus among believers concerning any other part of the view. Maybe the soul goes on to heaven or hell. Maybe it will survive in Abraham's bosom or Hades. Maybe interim existence is preferable to our current lives. Then again, maybe it's not preferable at all. To say the least, I find all of this to be highly contradictory.

While there is more that could be said about this perspective, everything we have covered so far in this chapter essentially builds towards this single point: if the so-called "traditional Christian view" (i.e. the *temporary-disembodiment position*, or the TDP) of the state of the dead is true, then Paul's case against the early Gnostic presence in Corinth (and elsewhere) sounds utterly absurd. He would essentially have been making it his mission to prove that "we" cannot exist without a body, only to later suggest that we can actually do so during the interim period. This is like someone saying, "I never, *ever* smoke . . . except between the hours of six and ten."

While being quite certain of their position, this is perhaps why the

---

[151] Ibid, 231.

proponents of the TDP admit that the biblical evidence in favor of this belief is left wanting. Moreland and Habermas candidly point this out for us, saying:

> "With the traditional view established as the best expression of the Christian understanding of the intermediate state for the believer in Christ, we can take a look at the nature of this disembodiment. What is it like? Unfortunately, when we look to the Bible for an answer, we find very little information. But from what little we can find, we learn some things about this state."[152]

To those in the fields of philosophy and apologetics, this type of argument displays a very common logical fallacy referred to as "circular reasoning." To put it succinctly, circular reasoning is simply the act of assuming the very argument you are trying to actually prove (i.e. beginning with the conclusion). In this case, they are attempting to show that the biblical view of the intermediate state is that the soul consciously lives without a body. However, their method of proving this assertion is to *assume* that this is the biblical perspective, even though the Bible contains "very little information" about this type of existence.

This argument would boil down to something like this: "how do we know that the TDP is the correct way to view the state of the dead? Well, we know because the TDP is the correct way to view the state of the dead." Apparently, the "traditional view" became traditional based on the scarcity of its biblical support. As I have said throughout this book, the reasons for believing that we will someday live as disembodied spirits is much more emotional than evidential. Many of us simply allow our desires to get in the way of what is most reasonable.

By all measures of logic and rationality, the conclusion of this matter should be obvious; within the TDP, the resurrection body is a completely dispensable feature in sustaining our lives after we die. The soul can function with or without the body. The difference is perhaps simply the *degree to which* it can function. Now, we once again find ourselves in familiar territory. We have another example of adding an ingredient to a recipe that doesn't call for it. The addition of the body to the soul is much like the addition of yellow food coloring to a glass of lemonade; the only thing that has actually changed

---

[152] Ibid. 231.

is the value of the color. The lemonade is now "more yellow," I suppose. If we are able to sufficiently function in the afterlife without a body, then why do we need one at all? According to the TDP, we need a physical and immaterial component to exist in this age *and* the next; except, quite conveniently, during the time between our deaths and our resurrections. For that period of time, our souls become consciously self-sufficient on their own. They are not before this earthly life, nor are they in the ultimate sense. But during the interim period? You bet.

Finally, the case could perhaps be made that we only need the resurrection body when God's Kingdom arrives in its fullness. The new heavens and new earth will of course be substantive realities (as I have covered in detail). This being the case, it stands to reason that we will need to be substantive beings. This is probably much of what Paul meant in 1 Corinthians 15:50; in order to inherit the perfected physical Kingdom, we must first be given perfected bodies. Don't misunderstand me, I fully agree with Paul's words here. But this teaching does not make disembodied life during the interim period even the slightest bit more probable. In fact, the problems I have presented above remain completely unresolved. The previous argument only proves the point that we will receive spiritual bodies at the resurrection, which is squarely placed at the end of the age and at Christ's return. The entire issue is still about what happens during the time between this tangible existence and the next.

At this point, I feel the need to repeat something that I previously said. I have learned much from the people I have referenced in this chapter (and elsewhere), and I certainly respect both their intellects and their contributions to God's Kingdom. But as far as the topic of this book is concerned, I simply find their views to be incomplete. Any doctrine that imagines the soul as a self-sufficient being that is capable of living on its own will fall victim to marginalizing the necessity of the body. Try as they might to avoid it, temporary-disembodiment advocates end up promoting a view of the body-soul relationship that sounds more like the Gnostic or Platonic variety than the biblical variety.

Even the highly-esteemed theologian Thomas Aquinas—while holding to something like the TDP—could not help but ultimately view the body as a hindrance to the soul, saying, "Wherefore just as a body is conveyed at once to its place . . . so too the soul, the *bonds of the flesh* being broken, whereby *it was detained* in the state of the way, receives at once its reward or punishment . . ..

"[153] The truth is clear; in order to believe that the human soul consciously survives the death of the body, one *must* denigrate the necessity of the body in the process. While Plato had no problem doing so, Paul, Jesus, and all others whose words are recorded within the Bible certainly did. With all of this being said, turnabout is fair play. It would be unreasonable for me to throw stones at particular views of the afterlife without attempting to have a better answer to the question. I believe this is where my views on the matter can shed some light on the situation. But I must first rehash a tradition of thought that is similar, but certainly not identical, to my own.

THE SLEEP-DEATH TRADITION

At the onset of this book, I discussed the fact that there is a third option within Christian thought concerning the afterlife and the state of the dead. This option is the one that most people within the church never talk about, and many have never even heard of. Historically, this view has been referred to as the doctrine of *soul sleep*. I recall a discussion I had with a professor and some classmates during my undergraduate studies. The subject du jour was actually the topic of this book: the state of the dead. While everyone in the room affirmed that the souls of deceased Christians are presently living in either heaven or Abraham's bosom (not that they made a distinction between the two), I quietly voiced my concerns about that notion. Mind you, this was long before I actually knew exactly what I believed about the matter. But suffice it to say that the traditional view of things just never sat well with me. Not on this issue, at least. It always had an odor of absurdity to it.

After the room went silent because I had dared to question the status quo—the very thing we are all taught in Sunday school from day one—one person spoke up, and I'll never forget what he said. To paraphrase, he said: "You are promoting the doctrine of soul sleep. That is a heretical view, and true Christians don't believe it. What you're saying is actually dangerous." So, there it was: the first time I had heard about the doctrine of soul sleep. That was the day that the view I suspected to be true actually met its name. That was the day that I learned about one of the "dirty little secrets" in the church. Of course, it was also the day I realized that I was some sort of "heretic" because my beliefs about the state of the dead just didn't pass the theological sniff-test to those who had always been steeped in church doctrine. I suspect

---

[153] Thomas Aquinas, *Summa Theologica*, 6373-74, (emphasis mine).

Paul felt the same way in his day, and Tyndale in his. Years later, I have a lot better idea about why I do not consent to the way of thinking most everyone else does on this particular issue. But I also have a better idea about why I do not hold all of the same views that are often connected with the doctrine of soul sleep. I would now like to recap some very important issues, and also further explain why I have dared to challenge "tradition."

There are several major points to consider when evaluating the basic tenets of the sleep-death tradition. The first point to consider has to do with a belief that has surfaced all throughout this book: the immortality of the soul. While this view has dominated much of church history and is vital to the TDP—whether its adherents realize/admit it or not—there are serious problems with this belief. In order for the immortality of the soul to be true, the physical and spiritual makeup of human beings must allow it. But alas, they do not. What I mean is this: if a human soul is going to be "immortal," and later live by itself after the expiration of the body, then the soul would necessarily need to be its own being. The soul would essentially be a "ghost within the machine," so to speak. The problem is that the very Scriptures Paul and the New Testament authors relied so heavily upon (the Old Testament writings) don't allow this as a possibility. The Hebrew term that we often translate as "soul" (*nepesh*) never refers to something resembling the immortal soul or an immaterial person that can subsist independent of the body.[154] As I have pointed out throughout this book, this is neither biblical nor rational.

The second point serves a more personal, but equally important role. While I agree that the state of the dead is an unconscious one, the doctrine of soul sleep lends itself to the very same problem as the immortality of the soul—the name alone suggests that a human soul is something that could potentially do anything, like "sleep," in and of itself. The name suggests an unwarranted division between the body and the soul, as the soul goes on to "sleep" while the body is gone. Though the basic tenets of soul sleep remain true, it was right for its adherents to search for another description. For this reason, the move by some to calling this doctrine *Christian mortalism* seems to have been much more fitting. Today, it is more common to hear the term *conditional immortality* (or *Christian conditionalism*) in association with many of the beliefs held within these perspectives.

While I agree with some of the basic tenets of conditional immortality, I also feel as though the name itself does not entirely reflect the beliefs held

---

[154] Glenn Andrews, "What Is Conditional Immortality?"

within it. The problem is that mortality is not "conditional," as the name clearly suggests. Certainly, the mortality of the human body is undeniable; our bodies will be rendered obsolete after death, as a new body is required if we are to exist for the rest of eternity in the Kingdom of God (1 Cor. 15:50-54). At the same time, the human soul is not subject to *conditionally* living on or dying—at least not at the "first death." It is just as Jesus so famously said: "Do not be afraid of those who kill the body but cannot kill the soul. Rather, be afraid of the One who can destroy both the body and the soul in hell" (Mt. 10:28). In Scripture, the death of the soul is always associated with the "second death."

Jesus was clear that the body can be destroyed by either human or naturalistic causes, but the soul can only be destroyed by a divine sentence to Gehenna (Mt. 10:28). But doesn't this suggest the idea that, contrary to the perspective I have put forth throughout the entire book, the soul actually is an immaterial being that can exist apart from the body? In short, no. Rather, we might view this in the following way: the "first death" is the extinguishment of life in this world, and the "second death" is the ultimate punishment and *destruction of our identities* once and for all. Leaving life in this world is to die, but leaving life in the next is to become extinct. This does not mean that the soul is immortal. It is not a separate being that can function in any capacity apart from the body, nor does it exist prior to the time we are conceived, as many ancient Greek philosophers alleged. And this is where I even find fault with the soul sleep views previously mentioned.

On the whole, these views still make the soul sound like an independent being that will one day go on to exist (unconsciously) somewhere else. Besides the clear difference that the soul is unconscious during the interim period, the overall ideas about what the soul actually is are not overly different than those found within the TDP. In other words, even the soul sleep traditions do not take a stern enough stance against the type of body-soul dualism that is at play within those views that affirm conscious, disembodied existence. The soul is still an independent being, of sorts. There is still the "ghost within the machine" in many respects, it's just that the ghost does not consciously live without the body. While I share in the basic belief that the dead are not consciously living somewhere, my view is by no means a carbon copy of the various soul sleep doctrines. Far from it. With this brief clarification about the ideas and terminology represented within the sleep-death tradition, we are prepared to evaluate my view in greater detail.

IDENTITY INFORMATION

At this point, we have taken a tour through the biblical and historical maze of the afterlife. I say "maze" because it is clear how many false paths and dead ends one can reach in evaluating the logistics of life after death. At the same time, there is one route through the twists and turns that appears to make the best sense of the problem—the one that views death as an unconscious period of time (Paul's "sleep") prior to the general resurrection. This is the basic premise behind the doctrine of soul sleep, and also of more contemporary views like *Christian mortalism* or *Christian conditionalism*. But in my mind, none of these views (nor any others that I know of) discuss the nature of the soul as it truly is.

We know that the body is not the connection between this life and the next because all bodies will utterly decay over time, yet the Bible is clear that there is a connection between our lives now and our lives in the next age. We have also seen that the soul must be the connection between the two, but the Bible is clear that it is not "us" in a spirit form that will later go on to live on its own. The soul is the tie that binds this life to the next, but it is not a being unto itself. So, what in the world is the soul? In no uncertain terms, *the soul is information*: not a being or a naked spirit of sorts, but information.

Before getting into the details about my perspective that the soul is actually a type of information, I feel that for clarity's sake it is necessary to briefly address the logistics of each view of the afterlife that we have assessed throughout the book. Recall that there are three general possibilities for believers concerning the state of the dead in Christian thought. The first is that we immediately depart to heaven when we die. We would go to heaven as disembodied spirits, though a small percentage of people hold that this could occur with a resurrection body (the *immediate resurrection position*).[155] The second possibility is that our souls could consciously depart to the realm of the dead, as some see in Abraham's bosom or Sheol/Hades. The final view is that we could remain in an unconscious state of being after death until the resurrection, in which the soul returns to God and the body returns to the ground. Realistically, only the first two general views hold to the belief in the

---

[155] In my estimation, there is very little reason to hold to this idea. Clearly, the reception of the resurrection body is one of the key issues involved with Christ's return. Hence, that cannot happen at death.

immorality of the soul, though nearly all (*recreationists* aside)[156] would typically hold to at least some type of body-soul dualism.

To simplify this a bit, most theologians agree—and have agreed throughout history— that the body and the soul are separate components that together comprise a living being. "Substance dualism" entails the belief that the soul (or the "mind") can live independent of the body, which clearly makes it more important than the body in my estimation. Substance dualism is essentially the backbone of Platonic thought on these issues, and also of any view that the soul consciously survives the death of the body. While I do not believe that the Bible supports this view, we would go too far to say that all forms of body-soul dualism are incorrect. The Bible is clear that there is a body and there is a soul, and they are not the same thing. I discuss my own view of how I see this relationship working later in this section.

Greek philosophers like Plato—whom, admittedly, I have criticized rather harshly throughout this book—were not *entirely* wrong on this issue. The idea that human beings are not wholly reducible to material causes— "we" are not simply our brains—seems utterly necessary if there is going to be a genuine connection between this life and the next. This is one place where "tradition" has it right. The point of divergence has to do with our definitions of what the "soul," the "mind," or what have you, actually is. The first two general views of the afterlife ascribe to the belief that the soul is capable of conscious existence by itself, while the last view holds that the human soul is not capable of consciously existing apart from its union with a physical body. This being said, the overall sequence of events will essentially be the same in the first two views but not the third. In light of this point, I will be evaluating the first two views together because they require the exact same types of events; in essence, both are possibilities within the TDP, though I have already discussed the problems with lumping them together in order to prove a common view of the afterlife.[157] For simplicity's sake, I will now call the first two views "scenario (A)," and the third view "scenario (B)." Now, let's take a look at how these scenarios flesh themselves out in reality.

---

[156] The *recreation* view holds that humans beings completely die (i.e. become "extinct") at death, and are completely recreated—body and soul together—at the general resurrection. In truth, this is probably closer (though not identical) to my own view than any others I have mentioned.

[157] Revisit the last section of chapter three, entitled "A Foot in Each Door," for clarification of this point.

Imagine all of the steps that must occur in scenario (A) during the process of getting believers into their ultimate dwelling place, the new earth.

1) We die, and our souls return to God while our bodies return to the ground.
2) There, we are judged in order to determine where we will spend our lives before the general resurrection.
3) After "particular judgment," we are sent to either Abraham's bosom or heaven.
4) In one of these two realms, we live in a very hazy (but conscious) state of existence until the return of Christ.
5) When Christ does return to earth, the righteous will be given resurrection bodies, and he will judge us *again*. This time, the judgment will determine where we will spend the rest of eternity.
6) At this point, the living would be given the resurrection body and be caught up to meet Christ for the inauguration of the "millennial reign," (however one wishes to view that time).[158]
7) Finally, God will destroy Satan and the forces of evil, and we will then be set to reign with Christ in a world of everlasting peace and security (the new heavens and new earth).

Within this view, there are two different judgments. This is problematic because the Bible only definitively speaks of one (which I previously discussed). Furthermore, there are three different modes of existence—one as a disembodied soul, and two as a soul living in union with a body. Of those, only the latter are biblical views of the body-soul relationship. Additionally, it is apparent that there are at least seven steps in this particular scenario. This perspective likens the soul to a rubber ball that has been thrown into a confined room; *here* it is (earth), then *there* it is (Abraham's bosom/heaven), then *there* it goes again (the millennial reign), then it finally comes to rest (the new heavens and earth). Bounce . . . bounce . . . bounce goes the soul.

What if scenario (B) is true though? Does the third general view, the one that I am advocating in this book, make better sense of things? Let's evaluate it and see.

---

[158] See Clouse's article "Millennium," in *The Evangelical Dictionary of Theology*, 770-74, for a thorough assessment of the various views of the millennial reign.

1) We die, and the soul returns to God while the body returns to the ground.

2) From there, nothing happens for an unknown period of time. (This is true from our perspective anyway, being that we don't know when Christ will return.)

3) Whenever he does return, we are judged for the first (and only) occasion. At that time, our souls (identity information) are united with resurrection bodies, and we proceed to reign with Christ during the millennium.

4) Lastly, Christ defeats the forces of evil once and for all, and we go on to reign with God in the new heavens and new earth.

While this series of events is clearly less confusing—there are four steps rather than seven—it is actually even more simplistic than it appears.

We must remember that the events in scenario (B) occur in reality, but they do not occur from the standpoint of personal perception. That is, the temporal aspect of the intermediate state is real from the perspective of the living but not from that of the dead. In all, we essentially have only two *conscious* movements: from our last conscious moments on this earth, to our first conscious moments with Christ at his return. It's that simple. Notice also that there is only one judgment, which is actually spoken of throughout the Bible. Likewise, there is only one resurrection: the *general one*, which is also clearly defined in Scripture. Furthermore, there is only one true mode of existence—the body and soul unity that both the Old and New Testaments consistently portray as reality. During the period between these two movements, there is no "time"—we will not know a thing about it. Our bodies will return to the earth, where they will decay like everyone else's. Our identity information (the soul), however, will return to God. With its Creator, it will not "die," "sleep," or continue in conscious "immortality" as other doctrines have asserted. Again, these things could only occur if the soul were itself a living being. But it isn't. The soul is half of the equation that makes a living person.

Apart from its union with a body, the soul can do nothing (consciously) whatsoever in and of itself. This does not mean that it is deceased or that it goes extinct at death, either. Those words describe something that happens to living persons or creatures, not to a component of persons or living creatures. But the soul does continue to exist in very important ways, which I will discuss momentarily. The most important feature of my view, in terms of the events described above, is that it eliminates many problems that exist within the more common views. While scenario (A) makes our souls into beings that fly all over the place like a game of "soul ping pong," my view, which exists within the scenario (B) views, is much less exhausting. As far as our own conscious perspectives are concerned, we simply go from existing in this world to existing in the next. We go from this age to the next. We go from this physical mode of existence to the perfected mode of existence: body, world and all. There is no concern for what could be happening during the intermediate state.

As evidenced throughout the book, this cuts off an enormous number of complexities that may or may not be occurring during the interim period. I think of Purgatory, the so-called "Harrowing of Hell," the events surrounding the resurrections of people like Lazarus and Jairus' daughter, the uncertainty of what "paradise" is, and the overall debate concerning the way in which our disembodied spirits presently live (which is the major topic of the next chapter) in the meantime, just to name a few.

Having discussed how much less baggage we would have to carry if we accepted my view as being valid, I now want to finish up this section by talking about why this view is not just another in the line of soul sleep doctrines. The first thing I would like to mention is what the identity information view *is not*. It is not contrary to all views of body-soul dualism, which generally involves a commitment to the idea that there is an immaterial aspect of our humanity, and that it is unique from the physical aspect. I certainly reject substance dualism because it involves the idea that the soul can consciously exist apart from the body. For identical reasons, I reject the immortality of the soul. But neither do I support a monistic view that seeks to make the body and the soul into identical (and merely physical) items, nor do I agree with the idea that the whole being (body and soul) goes *extinct* at death.

As I have discussed in detail, the Bible is clear that there will be continuity between who we are now and who we will be after the resurrection. For this reason, I do believe in what is called "property dualism." Essentially, this is the view that while there is only one type of substance in the world (the physical kind), there are two different types of properties (physical and mental). Applied to our subject, this means that while there is no soul within us that can live apart from the body, there is still an immaterial aspect to our existence. There is no conscious soul living inside of us, but there is identity information associated with us. Like all other types of information, it is not material or something that can be grasped. But it most certainly does exist.

Like ideas or numbers, the soul (identity information) is real, but it is not tangible or substantive.

Moving on from the deep philosophy stuff for the time being, I most definitely do not believe in particular views of *annihilationism*—which often come part and parcel with most other views of an unconscious interim period. This view essentially asserts that the unrepentant are "annihilated" after the judgment rather than undergoing any truly lasting punishment and estrangement from God. I think a very good case can be made that the unrepentant actually will become extinct at some point, but only after they have received the due punishment for their rebelliousness. In that sense, the doctrine of annihilationism could be seen as being accurate. However, the idea often posited by annihilationists that "hell" is simply a blazing fire where the wicked are instantaneously destroyed cannot possibly be accurate.

While the details of my position on this particular point are better left for another time and place, I actually agree here with scholars like Moreland and Habermas that this form of annihilationism is not consistent with the biblical descriptions of hell.[159] Among other problems, there would not be a just judgment of all people in this view; we would not truly be rewarded or punished according to our own deeds, as Jesus makes certain in texts like Revelation 22:12 and within many of his parables. If that particular annihilationist perspective is correct, then Hitler would ultimately share an identical fate to those who simply lived shoddy lives of unbelief. Both are equally annihilated. Likewise, there would be no ultimate difference between someone who selflessly serves God their entire lives and the criminal who repents on his or her deathbed. None of these perspectives make logical sense of the afterlife, nor do they make sense of the overall message of Scripture.

Now, let's examine what the informational view of the soul says about our present and future conditions. Like some of the other thinkers I have mentioned, I still hold that the soul serves as the source of our characters, our memories, and our "selves." It isn't coincidental that another way of translating the word *psuche*—the New Testament term we typically translate as "soul"—is "self." In many ways, it is our own personal databank; it is everything that makes us, *us*. This is exactly why I feel comfortable referring to the soul as "identity information." During the interim period, the mortal body returns to the dust of the earth and the soul (the "identity information")

---

[159] See Moreland and Habermas' *Beyond Death*, 302-311, for a more detailed refutation of this view of annihilationism.

returns to God. At the resurrection, the identity information is united with our perfected bodies just as it once was with our corrupted ones. In this line of reasoning, one's personal "identity," or "character" if you like, somehow remains intact while the physical body is a new and improved creation.

With this being said, what is the most significant difference between my view that the soul is identity information and all of the other views? How can I hold that the soul goes on at death, even though I completely disagree with the TDP's premise that the soul consciously survives the death of the body? Aren't I contradicting the major premise of this book by saying that the soul continues to exist after we die, and that it serves as the source of our identities? Actually, not at all. Allow me to elaborate on what I have been saying in this section. The reason why there is no contradiction is that my view of the soul is radically different than others. Rather than viewing the soul as its own being—as "us" who is trapped within a body—I view the soul as information. Again, the soul is *information*. It is not just any kind of information, either. The soul is our *identity information*.

Because of this distinction—and this point cannot be emphasized enough—I do not believe the soul is a living being. When God creates our new bodies, He will unite the soul He has held on file with the new body. God will unite the software (the soul) with the new hardware (the resurrection body). God will unite the identity information with a spiritual body like that of Christ's. The result is a being of identical character that is capable of living for the rest of eternity in the new heavens and new earth. If you recall the previous chapter, this is completely consistent with what Jesus revealed to us through his resurrection. While the soul is the aspect of human existence that holds our personal information (or *is* our personal information), it is not itself a being, and so it cannot function apart from a body. This is why referring to the soul as the "real you" (or something similar) is radically different than affirming that the soul maintains our personal identities *in the context of its relationship to the body*. According to the TDP, the soul can consciously persist without the need for a body. In my view, the soul requires a body to function; to truly live and be the "real you," your soul must unite with a body. Again, the software and the hardware are interdependent components.

I know that many of you who are reading this will undoubtedly find my description of the relationship between the body and the soul difficult to swallow. Some of you will even feel as though it is scary or, as my college classmate put it, "dangerous." The desire to believe that there is an immaterial person living within our bodies—a "ghost behind the machine," an "inner being," a "real us," etc.—is something that has been ingrained into our brains for as long as most of us can remember. And yes, if the soul really is our identity information and not some separate being living within the body, the ramifications would be exceedingly significant. It will likely change much of what you believe about how everything in the world works. It certainly did for me. But before closing the book and simply trusting in what we have been coached to believe, it may surprise you to know that this view of the soul is actually completely consistent with all other aspects of reality.

For example, consider the immense amount of data that is constantly being sent, received, processed, and ultimately stored within our world. A study displayed in 2011 by the University of Southern California revealed some truly astonishing facts about the amount of data that has been created and stored by humanity. Martin Hilbert, the lead author of the article, summarized one of the key points as follows: "Looking at both analog and digital devices, the researchers calculate that humankind is able to store at least 295 exabytes of information. (Yes, that's a number with 20 zeroes in it)."[160] While the full article reveals the undeniable (but unmentioned) point that we were engineered by an unimaginably intelligent mathematician that theists call "God," this information also proves a very telling fact about the reality of existence—abstract or immaterial objects require physical substrates in order to exist. Data requires physical storage. In fact, data storage facilities of *immense* proportions exist all over the world.[161]

Data storage centers are not the only places where we find that information requires a physical substrate—and vice versa—in order to functionally exist. In 1953, James Watson and Francis Crick—the co-discoverers of the DNA double helix—revealed that DNA is structured in such a way that it can store information as a four-character digital code.[162] This "code" determines the way we develop, function, and reproduce. Prominent philosopher of science, Stephen Meyer, expounds upon the nature of the information found within DNA:

---

[160] Martin Hilbert, "How much information is there in the world?"

[161] For a few examples, consider several of the world's largest data storage centers. The data center in Chicago, IL, totals 1.1 *million* square feet of storage. The centers in Atlanta, GA, and Florida total 990,000 square feet and 750,000 square feet, respectively. For more information, see the *Mozy* article, "Where is the World's Data Being Stored?"

[162] Stephen C. Meyer, "Not by chance."

"After the early 1960's, further discoveries made clear that the digital information in DNA and RNA is only part of a complex information processing system—an advanced form of nanotechnology that both mirrors and exceeds our own in its complexity, design logic and information storage density."[163]

Have you ever thought about how strange all of this really is? As we are all aware, we cannot hold information with our hands; information is simply not a tangible reality. Yet, it powers our world and indeed the universe around us. It runs our computers, powers our digital devices, explains our languages, codes for our DNA, and so much more. Even our identities are comprised of information, and that information is called the "soul." While I understand that this could strike many readers as being odd, we should not feel in any way uncomfortable about thinking of the soul as "identity information" and our bodies as the "data carriers." Truth be told, we understand all other aspects of reality in precisely the same way.

Apart from the biblical evidence discussed throughout this book, there is also an unavoidable argument from both logic and experience that validates the interdependent relationship between the body and the soul: our personalities change over time. "We" change over time. This is true with regards to both our physical appearances and our personal identities. There can be no doubt among thinking people that the physical realities of this world help to shape our characters throughout the course of our lives. Where you were born, with whom you lived, the types of trials you went through, the people you associated with, the physical harm you endured throughout life, and so forth, all directly affect your personal identity. The same is true for all of us. We experience this reality, and we logically know it to be true. While this much is undeniable, it becomes theologically problematic when we begin speaking in terms of dying and "going to heaven," for example. What, or *who*, exactly is it that is supposed to be going to heaven? It can't be the body; our bodies will end up in either crematoriums or caskets. If it is not the earthly body that goes on, then it must be the soul.

While this may seem like a simple observation, it opens the door to some of the most difficult questions we could ever imagine. When a person has lived well into adulthood before passing away, his or her identity has been

---

[163] Ibid.

extensively developed prior to their departure from this world. But what if someone dies, Lord forbid, prematurely? The person—body, soul, identity, and all—someone is as a child is *drastically* different than the person they are as an adult.

You may already see the problem here. Who "we" are depends stringently upon how long we have lived and what has occurred during that time. I was different at five years old than I later was at ten years old, and different at seventeen than at thirty, and so forth. So were you. So is everyone. The unavoidable question, then, is this: what version of "us" goes on into the afterlife? Are some eternally destined to be perpetual, immature six-year-olds? Will those who tragically die before reaching adulthood remain as children forever? Will those who succumb late in their lives to devastating mental illnesses like Alzheimer's disease or the various types of dementia carry that version of themselves into the next age? Make no mistake about it: these questions present all of us with a number of very difficult considerations, and it would be an act of sheer hubris to suggest that I have all of the answers to these problems. But even the basic observation that the nature of the human soul—the component of our personal identities—is inextricably connected to the human body and our various substantive circumstances indicates something *extremely* important. Specifically, it reveals to us that any view that treats the human soul as the "real being" or the human body as something of secondary importance fails to adequately account for this connection. As I discussed in the two sections directly preceding this one,[164] the TDP unavoidably makes this mistake.

The observation that our physical bodies directly dictate our personal identities further illustrates why we should think of the soul in terms of identity information, and not as its own conscious being that is contained within a body (as the TDP essentially suggests). The human soul is the data that connects the natural body and the spiritual body; it is the tie that binds life in this age to life in the next. If the soul is viewed in this way, then the "entire you"—the sum of all life experiences—is what is stored by God at death. It is not the two-year-old "you," the seventy-two-year-old "you," the "you" with Alzheimer's, or the "you" at the pinnacle of your intellectual prowess. Rather, "you"—and who "you" will be at the resurrection—are a complete composite of your entire life's story. *You are the sum of your experiences.* This also means that, even when we are raised from the dead and given new bodies,

---

[164] I am referring to the sections entitled "Just Add Body" and "Why Add Body?"

we will continue to experience new things and grow as individuals. Our identities will continue to develop. It stands to reason that the same is already true of the angelic beings. While we are still discussing the significance of the informational view of the soul, let's consider one more place where this particular view can help us to make sense of another difficult issue.

One of the greatest philosophical and theological issues theists have ever faced is the issue of ensoulment, or the origin of the soul. When, *exactly*, does God give each one of us a soul? Historically, several options have been suggested as solutions to this question. In particular, the doctrines of *traducianism* and *creationism* have been the two most prominent views. In short, traducianism is the view that the soul is the product of human procreation; God initiated life (the soul) with Adam, and that life is transferred to every human being since then without direct divine intervention. Alternatively, creationism is the view that every human soul is directly created by God, either at conception or some point thereafter. Neither view is perfect—chiefly because both views wrongly equate the breath of life, or the animating source of the body, with the soul—but creationism seems to have significantly more downfalls.

If ensoulment occurs at the moment of conception, then God must be jumping in to insert a soul into every human being that has, is, or will ever live. But where was the soul prior to that? Does God have a bunch of blank souls on tap, or is God creating one from scratch every time fertilization occurs? What if that child is conceived by rape, or a milder form of contact (like unlawful sexual relations)? God would have to be somehow involved in the situation, certainly. Worse, what if the person is physically doomed from the beginning, being severely predisposed to (or already possessing) a horrible disease of some sort? God could be providing a soul to someone who is going to suffer throughout their entire lives, or someone who won't even make it past the first trimester. If this seems a little messier than what we should feel comfortable with, it's because it is.

On the other hand, what if God provides the soul well after conception? If true, each of us would be a conscious human being while having only a body, prior to ensoulment. We would not need a soul to live in this case, which is the opposite problem I pointed out concerning the TPD, which posits that we don't actually need a body to function. If we can operate without a soul, then why do we need one? I guess I would have to write a new section entitled, *Just Add Soul!* Clearly, the prospect of post-conception ensoulment is of no help. Finally, the soul could hypothetically exist prior to conception. This is, of course, one of the grand claims couched within the belief in the immortality of the soul. But if this is true, then all of us would essentially be pre-existent and eternal; we would basically be just like God. If we indeed possess souls that can consciously exist apart from the body, there doesn't seem to be any remotely logical way out of the mess. Ensoulment simply poses too many problems, regardless of how we might look at it.

But what if the soul is not actually some being that can consciously exist with or without the body? What if it is, as I propose, identity information? If the soul is the data of the sum of our life experiences, then there is no moment of divine ensoulment. God does not reach in and plug a soul into each person at some unknown, and undeniably problematic, point in time. Rather, the soul begins to exist at the precise moment that the body does. The body and the soul are co-emergent. Your life's story started at the moment you were conceived, and it will continue accumulating until death. In some sense, traducianism is close to being correct about how this works out. The soul is the product of procreation; we all have identity information at the moment of conception.

However, the soul is not the driving force of the body. As I have mentioned throughout the book, it is the Spirit of God who initiated life for all people at the creation of Adam. This "breath of life" is perpetuated through human reproduction, and with every human being that enters the world, there is unique identity information (a "soul"). Moreover, if the soul is your identity information and not an independent being, then all of the problems mentioned above simply pose a much lesser threat to rationality. In fact, most of the problems with ensoulment cannot even pertain to this view of the soul, in principle. Perhaps it is not that all of the theories of ensoulment are fatally flawed, but that our definition of the soul has prevented any of them from being logically coherent. Maybe we have always been trying to fit a square peg into a round hole. I believe our views of the interim period and the afterlife in general are similar attempts at combining two ideas that simply cannot mesh: the necessity of physical existence with the idea of a soul that doesn't require such a thing.

Admittedly, the way in which God will work every last detail of this out remains at least somewhat of a mystery. I can accept that. But this makes much better sense than believing that the human identity in the next age is completely predicated on who each of us was on the day we died. What if someone dies after sustaining life-altering brain damage? Is that reflective of who he or she will be for the rest of eternity? Thankfully, it is not: *if* we are willing to reject the TDP and begin to view the soul as identity information rather than as some type of "ghost within the machine." Maybe, just maybe, the information view is what Paul was pointing towards in 1 Corinthians 15, when he spoke of the connection between the natural body and the spiritual body. It is also another reason why "spiritual existence" can *never* be separated from physical existence.

Some have offered that Paul intended the comparison between the earthly body and the resurrection body to be taken in its most literal sense. William Lane Craig makes this case, saying, "The resurrection body is not some different body. It is this body transformed into a glorious, immortal, Spirit-filled, incorruptible form. So if we received our resurrection body immediately upon death, the graves of all the Christians would be empty!"[165] While he is right that we do not receive our resurrection bodies at the moment of death (i.e. the *immediate resurrection position*), the view that God simply recycles our earthly body cannot be logically true. It's simply not possible that our earthly bodies will be literally and physically connected to the spiritual bodies we will one day receive, since so many bodies will have completely deteriorated by the time of the resurrection. If there is any sort of *physical* continuity, it could only come about if God chose to create a new body that would somehow resemble the old. While this is perhaps possible, the point remains the same—the resurrection body is not a restoration project, but a new creation. You cannot restore something that has completely deteriorated, nor can you restore something that has already become part of something else (like ashes in the sea).

God might *recreate* a body that no longer exists, but He cannot *restore* one. That would be like trying to restore a house that has already been bulldozed to the ground and scattered to dust. Simply pointing to Jesus' body as evidence that the natural body is literally made into the new one won't work in this particular case, either. Jesus' body remained in the tomb for "three days" (and not even three twenty-four hour periods, at that), and the missing body was crucial evidence that he had indeed conquered the grave. Jesus' earthly body must have been absent from the tomb, lest the resurrected Jesus be completely disassociated with the one who had entered the tomb. As the book of Acts records (from Psalms 16:10) concerning the messiah, "You

---

[165] William Lane Craig, "What Happens When We Die?"

will not let your holy one see decay" (13:35). Jesus was a special case. His body was not left in the grave to deteriorate like most others.[166]

With all of this being considered, Paul's use of the "seed" analogy in 1 Corinthians must not be taken *too* literally (15:37-38). Still, there is a connection between this life and the next; otherwise, Paul would be a liar, and the descriptions of Jesus' resurrection body would be extremely misleading (if not completely false). If the source of this continuity is not the overlap between this actual body and the next, then it must have to do with the soul. If my perspective about the function of the soul is close to being correct, then we may have our answer. The *entire mode of existence* is changed from the present one to the future, not simply the physical body. If this is indeed what Paul intended, it makes a great deal of sense. Jesus' resurrection body is the pattern for our own (1 Cor. 15:49), and his resurrection appearances are completely consistent with this perspective.

We have to remember that Jesus' physical appearance was never once the determining factor in others' ability to recognize him after the Resurrection. Mary Magdalene initially thought Jesus was the gardener (of all things), and only realized it was him when he succinctly called to her (Jn. 20:11-18). Jesus walked (and talked) the entire seven-mile trip from Jerusalem to Emmaus with two of his disciples without them realizing it was him. Only when he performed his familiar style of blessing the meal did they understand his identity (Lk. 24:13-35). Even the apostles, who had spent perhaps more than three consecutive years with Jesus, failed to physically recognize him when he appeared at the Sea of Galilee; only when he provided a miraculous catch did they grasp who he was (Jn. 21:1-14). In fact, even after seeing Jesus up close and speaking with him, the apostles considered (but didn't dare) asking him to reveal his identity to them![167]

Other examples could be mentioned, but the point should be clear. Jesus proves that we are very much like our old selves after we are raised from the

---

[166] Of course, many bodies are turned to dust in the act of cremation. Many people even choose to have their ashes spread at sea or elsewhere. How is God going to transform that?

[167] "Jesus said to them, 'come and have breakfast.' None of the disciples dared ask him, 'Who are you?' They knew it was the Lord" (Jn. 21:12). Clearly, it at least seemed rational to the disciples that they needed to verify that the man they were about to eat with was actually Jesus. John would never have added this detail if the issue had been crystal-clear. The point being, his closest companions did not even physically recognize him after seeing him multiple times face to face.

dead. But if we are expecting this to be largely based on physical appearances, then we may be sorely mistaken. In Philippians 3:21, Paul said that God will ". . . transform our lowly bodies so that they will be like his glorious body." The Greek term used here for "transform" (*metaschematisei*) means to "change the outward appearance (the dress, the form of presentment) of something."[168] This makes a great deal of sense when we consider Jesus' resurrection body. Jesus' personality had not changed, but his outward appearance certainly had. If the physical body is not the direct connection between the people we are now and the people we will be after the resurrection, then the continuity must be the soul, which I feel to be synonymous with the "identity information." This does not by any means lead us to conclude that the body is inferior to the soul *because both components are necessary* for conscious (real) existence. A soul without a body is like a program without a computer to run on.

Hypothetically speaking, this means that if God chose not to give us new bodies then we would never exist again. Our information may be either held or destroyed, but we would never again be conscious, living beings. In this, I am reminded again of a few of Jesus' more famous words of caution: "Do not be afraid of those who kill the body but cannot kill the soul. Rather, be afraid of the One who can destroy both soul and body in hell" (Mt. 10:28). Jesus was warning that we should not be afraid of those who can destroy us in our present state, but to be afraid of the One who can destroy us in our future state. Only God could completely erase our identities. In the end, it is this understanding of the nature of the human soul and its connection to the body that separates my view of identity information from the others. Most importantly, I believe that this perspective aligns more closely with Scripture and the overall logic of these issues than any other view that I know of.

To cap off this discussion, there are a few crucial features to understand about my view. For the purposes of clarity and simplicity, I have ordered these points in a numerical list.

1) It opposes the view that the soul "sleeps," "dies," or does any activity by its own power. As the immaterial aspect of a living being, it is not "immortal" because it is not its own being.
2) It accepts a commitment to property dualism, rejecting the monist perspective. The soul exists and is something "other than" the body. The soul has its own property, but not its own substance.

---

[168] Strong's Concordance, BibleHub.

3) It is firmly rooted in the biblical concept of body-soul unity, and the belief that both elements are required for us to be living beings in this world and the next.

4) It is almost entirely opposed to the *temporary-disembodiment position* (the TDP), which is frequently characterized as being the "traditional Christian view."

5) It holds that the soul is the source of personal information, or the "identity information." It is the link between this existence and the next, because while the resurrection body will be a brand new one, the identity will not. As such, the identity information returns to God where it is held on file until the day comes that God provides the soul with a glorified physical counterpart. Then, and only then, will we be living beings again. In this way, the continuity between this life and the next remains completely intact.

Here, I have attempted to provide as clear an understanding of my perspective as possible. I believe that this view not only adequately explains the overall scriptural account of the afterlife, but also radically simplifies many of the philosophical problems associated with any discussion about the state of the dead.

To be sure, a view is not superior to others merely by virtue of its simplicity, but by the sum of all its parts. There are, however, far fewer problems and inconsistencies that must be juggled within this perspective because of its plainness. I suggest, then, that we remove those steps that are neither biblical nor rational. Why further complicate a subject that is already so complex? This is particularly reasonable when we consider that the evidence in favor of purely immaterial realms of human existence is, to put it generously, far from overwhelming. In the final chapter of this book, I will seek to explain two very important questions that remain on the table, and I will do so in a rather concomitant manner. The first has to do with the underlying reasons why scholars and laypeople alike continue to opt for the more "traditional" view (the TDP) of the interim period, and the second is perhaps the most essential one for all of us at the present time—what relevance does all of this have here and now?

CHAPTER FIVE

WHAT DOES IT MATTER?

E very time I have ever taught students about the vast world of apocalyptic literature, I could count on there being at least a few questions about its relevance. I have fielded all sorts of questions. If we cannot know exactly when the world will end, why should we study the events surrounding it? Isn't all of this stuff completely up for debate? What on earth is an "eschaton?"[169] But I have most frequently heard this question: what does any of this have to do with our lives right now? All of these are fair questions, particularly because many churchgoers have been conditioned to believe that we can't make heads or tails of anything within the apocalyptic texts.

While certain groups have displayed a fanatical obsession with these writings, there truly seems to be a type of "apocaphobia" within other parts of the church. This is very unfortunate, particularly because the apocalyptic mindset permeates a considerable amount of what we read in the Old Testament (particularly in the prophets) and essentially everything we read about in the New Testament. Nevertheless, I understand that a theological endeavor that does not yield some type of practical application is difficult to swallow. I mean, either way we will be dead and gone, so what possible difference could it make to us right now? We either go on as a disembodied

---

[169] The "eschaton" comes from the Greek *eschatos*, which essentially means "last." This is where we get the term eschatology, which refers to the study of "last things." The eschaton is an umbrella term for all of the things that will happen at the end of the world. This would include the Parousia (the Second Coming), the judgment, the separation of the righteous and the wicked, the destruction of Satan, and others. Essentially, it is the climax of human history.

spirit at death, or we don't, but who cares? Contrary to popular opinion, I personally believe that apocalyptic literature has a great deal of practical application at the present. One such instance is actually the very topic of this book. While it can be challenging to see what possible relevance our views of the interim period could have on our lives now, there are a few ways in which it could have very real consequences.

GHOST STORIES

Ghost Hunters, Paranormal State, Ghost Stories, My Ghost Story, Ghost Adventures, The Dead Files, My Haunted House, Ghost Inside My Child, Paranormal Investigator, A Haunting, A Haunting in Connecticut, Long Island Medium, Ghost Mine, Haunted Collector and . . . well, you get the idea. Though the belief that human spirits interact with our world is far from knew, it has reached a fever pitch in American society over the last decade or so. The previous collection of TV shows and movies is just a sample of the massive list of "ghostly" entertainment that frequents our daily programming. Certainly, more are coming in the future. One of the most recent (2005) Gallop polls that inquired about the belief in ghosts revealed that roughly 75 percent of those interviewed believed in something we would consider to be paranormal.[170] More specifically, 37 percent of people believed that houses can be haunted, and roughly 32 percent of people believed that we can somehow encounter the ghosts or spirits of dead people in particular situations.[171] In 2006, when asking more than four thousand American teens about behaviors regarding the supernatural, the Barna Group found that an astonishing 73 percent of these teens admitted to having made some type of effort to contact spirits.[172] For Christian parents in particular, these numbers should be more than a little alarming.

Clearly, people of all faiths, ages, and backgrounds are fascinated with the prospect of ghosts. And why shouldn't we be? If the spirits of the dead can interact with us, then the possibilities would be endless. We could experience the people of the past and see the world, in some way, through their eyes. We could tell deceased loved ones how we feel about them, or even say our

---

[170] David W. Moore, "Three in Four Americans Believe in Paranormal."

[171] Ibid.

[172] Barna, "New Research Explores Teenage Views and Behavior Regarding the Supernatural."

final goodbyes. We could attempt to do what King Saul did with the prophet Samuel, and ask the fallen for guidance and counsel. Perhaps we could even obtain a bit of "beyond the grave" power to employ against our enemies. You name it, we could conceivably do it. All of this may sound appealing and, according to many worldviews, it is possible. The purpose of this book, however, is to assess our condition after death from a biblical perspective. Through this lens—the lens of the Judeo-Christian tradition—ghosts simply do not exist. While Christians can disagree on what happens when we die, we should not disagree on whether or not the spirits of the dead can contact the living. The reason for this is rather straightforward: every possible biblical doctrine of the afterlife essentially excludes this as a possibility.

Imagine once more that the TDP, at least its insistence that the soul can consciously survive on its own, is actually true. If so, then the souls of the deceased might venture to a place of comfort (Abraham's bosom, or even heaven) and the condemned would experience a place of torment (Hades or hell). If taken literally, the latter of these two possibilities is discussed in Jesus' parable of the Rich Man and Lazarus (Lk. 16:19-31). Since it represents the main (but not the *only*) source of evidence for this belief, we must discuss the ramifications of this view based on this story. As far as the issue of ghosts is concerned, there is one very crucial point that we must understand from the section, and it has to do with the rich man's request.

After fully realizing the type of destination that his chosen lifestyle had taken him, the rich man first asks Abraham to provide some type of relief. Apparently, even a few drops of water would help the situation (vs. 24). After failing to appease his own self-interests, he then moves to thinking about those whom he had left behind. Clearly, he was the same in death as he was in life. He proceeds to ask Abraham to send Lazarus back to warn his family, so that they may be spared the same fate. Abraham declines his request because they wouldn't believe it "even if someone rises from the dead." Abraham does not suggest to the man that such a thing—a spirit returning from the dead—is impossible, but I'm not sure he needed to. Even within the two realms of the story, there is said to be a "chasm" of separation that excludes physical contact as an option (v. 26). They are speaking from opposite sides of the intermediate realm, but they can do no more. If the dead cannot physically interact with the dead, then there is absolutely no reason to believe that the dead can do so with the living. At best, we could only assert that the dead can audibly communicate with us in some capacity (even this would be an unfathomable stretch). There would not, however, be the slightest chance of visible manifestation or physical contact. All of this, of course, is based on a literal reading of the parable. I have made it clear that I believe this story is thoroughly metaphorical in nature.

The conjuring of Samuel's spirit (discussed in chapter three) notwithstanding, such a possibility is scarcely imaginable within any other biblical passage. The apostles apparently did mistake Jesus for a "ghost" (*phantasma*), as recorded in Mark 6:49 and Matthew 14:26. This word is only used twice in the New Testament, and both instances are referring to the previous event. Such a thing is hinted at in Luke 24:37-39, where Jesus mysteriously appears to the apostles from nowhere. But the word used there is the much more common *pneuma* (spirit). This further illustrates that the word "ghost" is an anomaly that did not functionally mean anything strange or exotic to the biblical authors. This becomes even more apparent when we consider that the word *phantasma* essentially translates as "apparition." This being the case, the apostles simply believed that whatever they were seeing wasn't human because *humans* don't walk across the sea or appear out of thin air. The text should not be used to suggest that the apostles ascribed to a full-blown belief that dead human beings roam the earth. While such a notion probably existed on the fringe, it was certainly not part of the standard Jewish belief system.[173]

In all likelihood, the apostles were entertaining the idea simply based on the extreme nature of the events, not because they personally endorsed this way of thinking. Lastly, such a notion would be completely inconsistent with the overall view of the body-soul relationship that is depicted within the Bible. Suffice it to say that if spirits cannot even physically interact and "cross-over" between their respective realms, then why should we believe that they can cross the presumably greater divide and enter the realm of the living? They would need to, after all, if we were going to be able to see, touch, or tangibly experience them in any perceivable way. This, of course, is the very definition of a "ghost encounter."

Now, let's imagine that the departed enter into either heaven or hell immediately after death. While angels and demons are said to be able to act within this world (I discuss this again in the next section), dead human beings are not spoken of in this way. We already looked at the story of Samuel's spirit and the appearances of Elijah and Moses at the Transfiguration, but neither of these instances proves that dead beings can interact with the living

---

[173] Mike Uram, "Jewish Ghost Stories and the Walking Dead."

as a general rule. As we saw, the story of Samuel is littered with questions, so much so that we could ask whether or not "Samuel's spirit" was really him at all. Elijah was one of two people in the entire Bible who was truly assumed into heaven, and Moses may have been a rare exception based on his privileged place within the Old Testament narrative. Whatever the case may be, both were *physically* present with Christ anyway, and the situation served as an inauguration event; they are hardly examples of disembodied spirits coming back to interact with the living.

If we are to believe that the human soul goes to live in heaven at death, then it cannot be that we are changed (at that point) into angelic beings. Christ made it clear that such a transformation would only occur at the resurrection (Mk.12:25, Mt. 22:30). Though there is clear evidence that angels can interact with the living, those who have died are not—whichever way you look at it—angelic beings. This being the case, there simply isn't any biblical evidence of deceased people coming back to earth as disembodied spirits, if they were indeed living in heaven to begin with. Hence, contact with the living is not scripturally plausible on this front, either.

The final possibility, which I have advocated throughout this book, really doesn't need any additional analysis as far as ghosts are concerned. If my view that the soul is identity information (or any view ascribing to an unconscious interim period) is true, then there is literally no chance of the dead contacting the living in any capacity. The deceased are unconscious, so they certainly aren't gliding (or whatever ghosts would do) around our world. One can find my view to be in error, but they cannot disagree that it excludes the possibility of ghosts.

Whatever view of the afterlife we may choose to hold as Christians, it is apparent that ghostly activity is essentially (if not *entirely*) outside the bounds of human experience. Even if it were not, it was strictly forbidden to attempt to contact the dead in the Old Testament (Lev. 19:31, 20:6 and Dt. 18:9-14), and practices related to divination were certainly viewed negatively in the New Testament (Acts 16:16-18). Therein lies the problem. There is a very real sense in which entertaining the notion of ghosts ceases to actually be entertaining, as it may be in the movies, and begins to be a dangerous fascination. Those who choose to pursue ghosts are replacing worship with imagination, and are focusing their spiritual pursuits on something other than God. This, in and of itself, is a major problem: one that I will return to when I assess Purgatory in the next section. There are worse outcomes than this form of idolatry, however. A conversation I once had with a friend illustrates this grim reality quite well.

OTHER ENTITIES

A number of years ago, I decided to visit my friend Steven at his old farmhouse. Unfortunately, the visit did not go as planned because our discussion was continuously disrupted. These disturbances came in the form of knocks on a door, small whispering voices, creaks in the floorboards, and the like. Though I could ignore them at first, it became more and more obvious that these sounds were not common. At some point, I started to become a little alarmed. Steven, on the other hand, was not. He insisted that the noises were quite typical, and he believed that they could be attributed to a former relative who had died in the house years ago. He also informed me that he occasionally attempted to talk with this deceased relative; that's how sure he was about the entity's identity. I had my doubts, but did not press the issue.

Several months later, I received a call from my friend. But on this occasion, he was not his typically calm self. In a sort of frantic stutter, Steven explained that he had been pushed from behind while walking down his basement steps that very morning. If not for catching himself on the railing, he felt as though he could have been seriously injured during the experience. There were many steps, so it certainly would have been a long tumble to the bottom of his concrete basement. As you can imagine, I was pretty concerned about the situation. But the intriguing part of this story is that he was alone in the house. No one was there, nor had anyone been there all morning. There simply wasn't a rational explanation for his firmly-held belief that he had been pushed from behind. That was the day that Steven came over to my side of the fence on the ghost vs. "other entity" debate. Fortunately, the events that led him to this conclusion didn't cost him a trip to the ER (or worse).

The reason I say "other entity" is because there are two options here— angelic beings and demonic beings. As I discussed in the previous section, we are not dealing with the spirits of dead people. Steven's story is not unlike some of my own, or many others that I have heard about over the years. Most of you reading this have probably either had an experience like this or know someone who has. Certainly, the Bible is clear that angels and demons (who are fallen angels) can act within our world. There is a long history of God using angels to minster to His chosen servants (like Gideon, Mary, John, and Paul, to name only a few), and we already saw that Jesus and the apostles really did perform exorcisms. Though still mysterious in nature, angels certainly serve a positive role whenever they do interact with us. Besides the numerous times that angels deliver messages to God's servants, many people today attest to experiencing angelic beings in their own lives.

A pastor friend of mine, named Joe, once told me a fascinating story that I have never forgotten. While traveling home to visit relatives on one occasion, he and his brother found themselves in the middle of a very violent snow storm. To make matters worse, their car predictably began to stall until it finally broke down. With the snow swirling around them, and temperatures falling into dangerous lows, they became painfully aware that they were in serious trouble. Without cell phones (this was the late 1980's) or any nearby houses or towns, the situation had turned dire. But before the two men began to think about their final prayers, a truck appeared from behind the white chaos. From within the truck, a friendly face invited them into the warm interior. With no other options at their disposal, they happily jumped into the truck. During the drive to the nearest town, the three of them made pleasantries, but the man never formally introduced himself. While Joe and his brother found that to be somewhat strange, the circumstances certainly didn't lead them to worry too much about it.

Before entering into town, he revealed that he was the pastor of the town's largest church, pointing it out as they drove by. After stopping at one of the town's few motels, Joe and his brother settled in for the night. The following day, they were able to have their car towed to a nearby mechanic's shop to be fixed. Now that all was right with the world again, Joe and his brother decided to drive the rest of the way home later that day. Before leaving though, they thought it was only right to stop and thank the good pastor one last time. After arriving at the church, they searched for the mysterious man with no success. Finally, they asked some of the office staff where they might find him. At first, no one could put a name to the face, so Joe proceeded to describe the situation: snow storm, red pickup truck, an older, brown-haired man, and so on. After a long pause, a senior member of the church spoke up. She said to them, "Yeah, I recognize the man you're talking about—it sounds just like Pastor Brown!" Naturally, Joe was relieved that he might finally be able to find the man and thank him for what he had done. But before Joe was able to inquire about where he might presently find the pastor, the older woman added a haunting detail to her statement; "The man you're talking about can't be Pastor Brown, though—he's been dead for almost 15 years."

Though the previous story may seem rather fantastic to some, I have no reason to doubt that Joe was telling me the truth. Whether you believe that story or not, there is certainly a biblical and testimonial precedent for angelic intervention. For all the reasons discussed throughout this book, this could not have been the ghost of Pastor Brown. This was a physical being and a physical situation. Instead, the only explanation that makes sense is that they were dealing with a good celestial being that presented itself in a relatable way. To note this again, this does not suggest that angels are otherwise purely immaterial beings. There is much that we do not understand about the heavenly beings or the ways they could potentially present themselves to us. Besides, why would it be easier to take on some different appearance as an immaterial being than it would be as a material being? As an aside, I wonder the same thing about God with regards to the creation of the universe; why did God need to be "immaterial" in order to create a material world? Getting back to the point, an angel's ability to manifest itself in certain ways would actually be a physical feature of their existence rather than an immaterial one.

As in Joe's case, angelic encounters are always described in positive terms. As for demonic entities, well, not so much. It has been said that Satan's biggest trick is convincing the world he doesn't exist. I disagree with this statement for several reasons, but for one in particular. It seems to me that Satan (or a demon) is much more effective if he can convince us that he is essentially harmless. Better yet, if he can actually appear to be *good*. Satan wants us to worship him as we do God, after all. His goal, then, seems to be a reversal of the intended order; he wants us to believe that good is evil, and that evil is good. In the process of doing so, he shrewdly convinces us to do his will.

Just think about his encounter with Adam and Eve. By posing as one of God's "good" creations, he convinces the first couple to disobey God. And why? Because eating the fruit was actually a "good" thing. Satan convinced them that, despite what God had told them, they would benefit greatly from their decision to follow his advice. We see the same thing occur in all types of evil, from the cult leaders of the world like David Koresh and Jim Jones, to ruthless dictators like Hitler and Pol Pot. None of these individuals came out of the gate broadcasting their evil intentions. Rather, they sucked others in with their charm and charisma. Their schemes and their plans looked great . . . at first.

If this is true, what better way would there be to wreak havoc than to masquerade as someone we once knew, and were perhaps even very close to? Maybe this comes in the form of our beloved grandmother, an old friend, or perhaps just a deceased acquaintance. Whatever the case may be, buyer beware. Appearing in false forms is not at all out of character for Satan, as he has been disguising himself for eons. I just mentioned that his first known appearance in recorded history was in the form of one of God's many *good* creations—a serpent. Paul referred to Satan as the "angel of light" (2 Cor. 11:14), which suggests the ultimate example of the wolf in sheep's clothing mentality that the Bible frequently recognizes. This is proof enough that Satan doesn't wish to become invisible, but that he desires to blend into the crowd: to pass as one of the good guys. Though angels can manifest themselves in particular ways in order to positively affect us, the other side is undoubtedly playing a reciprocal role within the world. Steven wasn't dealing with the type of entity that wanted to save him from a snowstorm, but with the type that wished to see him tumble to his death.

The point is this: if we are encountering entities that we deem to be the spirits of deceased human beings, then we really need to watch our backs. As Steven's story indicates, this advice should be taken quite literally. Whether we are physically harmed or spiritually separated from God, falsely identifying otherworldly entities is a dangerous proposition. As the apostle John reminds us, we need to "test the spirits, for not all are from God" (1 Jn. 4:1). Put another way, your deceased aunt Belle means well—until she doesn't. The Bible's overall pessimism towards anything involving human spirits leads us further into some very controversial, but necessary, theological considerations. We must ask how else the beliefs and practices of the church have been influenced by this reality. There are certainly perspectives within parts of the church that take an enthrallment with human spirits to entirely different levels: levels that go far beyond your everyday "ghost walk." In some cases, spirits are considered to be our heavenly intercessors. Worse yet, they are sometimes even thought to be agents of salvation.

HAIL MIRAGE

Hail Mary, full of grace. The Lord is with thee.
Blessed art thou amongst women,
and blessed is the fruit of thy womb, Jesus.

Holy Mary, Mother of God,
pray for us sinners,
now and at the hour of our death. Amen.

At the beginning of this book, I mentioned that part (however large or small) of the problem between the Protestant Reformers and the Roman Catholic Church had to do with the state of the dead. In fact, Martin Luther's legendary "Ninety-five Theses," which historically marked the beginning of the Reformation, contained a lengthy refutation of the Catholic view of Purgatory.[174] Though the debate between Protestants and Catholics on the issue may have begun at this point in history, it certainly hasn't subsided. In general, Purgatory is viewed as a state of existence between this earthly life and the one that Christians will eventually enjoy for the rest of eternity. It is not, as some mistake it to be, an existence that all people will be required to experience. The Catechism of the Catholic Church succinctly discusses the purpose of Purgatory in the following way:

> "When the Lord comes in glory, and all his angels with him,
> death will be no more and all things will be subject to him.
> But at the present time some of his disciples are pilgrims on
> earth. Others have died and are being purified, while still
> others are in glory, contemplating 'in full light, God himself
> triune and one, exactly as he is.'"[175]

In this description, two major points become apparent. The first is the idea that believers can exist, at the present, in three distinct realties. We can be living on this earth, living in Purgatory, or perhaps even living in heaven with God. In this sense, the Catholic view of the interim period is somewhat of a hodgepodge of all available options, save for the possibility of unconsciously awaiting the resurrection. The second point revealed within the passage is that the very purpose of Purgatory is to "purify" deceased believers of their sins. While that much is apparent, the substance of what is being purified is much more ambiguous. As the view contends, there are particular types of sins that cannot be properly cleansed in this world and within the duration of the human life. Mentioning only Jesus' discussion

---

[174] Theses 10, 11, 15, 16, 17, 22, 25, 26, 27, 29 and 82 all mention Luther's disdain for the doctrine of Purgatory. "Luther's 95 Theses (A.D. 1512)."
[175] "Catechism of the Catholic Church." Online version, 249.

about blasphemy against the Holy Spirit, it is extremely unclear as to what other sins cannot be purified in this lifetime:

> "As for certain lesser faults, we must believe that, before the Final Judgment, there is a purifying fire. He who is truth says that whoever utters blasphemy against the Holy Spirit will be pardoned neither in this age nor in the age to come. From this sentence we understand that certain offenses can be forgiven in this age, but certain others in the age to come."[176]

One could discuss what other types of actions may be classified as sins that require future purification, but the point remains the same—Jesus' atonement is found to be insufficient in thoroughly cleansing all sins at the present. In other words, certain sins require something more than Christ's sacrifice in order to be completely removed.

In the case of Purgatory, these remaining sins require an unknown period of constructive punishment. So much for Romans 8:1, I suppose.[177] While this objection is quite serious on its own, the doctrine of Purgatory has more significant consequences concerning the state of the dead. The first, and most obvious, issue arising within this belief is that disembodied souls are able to exist in a place like Purgatory to begin with. Based on everything we have looked at concerning the nature of the body-soul relationship, this type of scenario ranges from highly unlikely to nearly impossible. But let's suppose for the moment that Purgatory actually reveals a genuine mode of existence after death. If true, there are naturally a number of implications worth discussing. Of these implications, the most significant is that Purgatory does not simply posit some type of closed realm for those souls being purified. Instead, it offers a point of contact between those souls and the "pilgrims on earth."

Within this relationship, we are able to affect those in Purgatory, and they are able to reciprocate. The question must naturally be raised, then: how can our actions affect those in Purgatory, and vice versa? Can we communicate with one another, pray for one another, or even make intercession for one

---

[176] Ibid. 269.

[177] "Therefore, there is now no condemnation for those who are in Christ Jesus." Apparently, some form of condemnation remains if a believer needs to enter into Purgatory.

another? The answer to all of these questions appears to be a resounding *yes*: The Church ". . . commends almsgiving, indulgences, and works of penance undertaken on behalf of the dead."[178] Moreover, "Our prayer for them is capable not only of helping them, but also of making their intercession for us effective."[179]

Where to begin? Let's start with the obvious and work our way down. The biblical negativity towards communicating with the dead is completely reversed in the doctrine of Purgatory, to the extent that it is actually encouraged. We are instructed to pray for the dead, to do all manner of charitable acts on their behalf, and we are even urged to perform acts of penance for them. As the previous account tells us, these actions are not simply goodwill gestures; they are thought to have a real impact on those who exist in that realm. Despite a lack of biblical support, it is believed that the dead can actually make atonement for the living as well.[180]

This moves us to another point. If salvation can be altered by others, in this life or the next, then Pandora's Box has officially been opened. Can believers apostatize (renounce their faith), live ungodly lives, or simply be noncommittal about God, then later be saved by the actions or prayers of the living? Can the actions or prayers of those in other realms, such as heaven or Purgatory, do the same for us? If so, then by what means and to what extent can this be accomplished? How much must we "get right" here on earth in order to reach either of these locations (by particular judgment), and how much must we do once we get there? For all we know, throngs of righteous souls could be working to secure your salvation as you read this! Imagine all the possibilities. Better yet, imagine all the questions this would leave us to entertain.

One thing seems apparent in all of this though—if salvation is not solely based upon the lives we lead here on earth, then the urgency of holy living dramatically plummets. Simply put, why do today what you (or someone else) could do tomorrow? In believing that the deceased can influence God's

---

[178] Ibid. 269.

[179] Ibid. 250.

[180] As described within the Catholic Catechism itself, the only New Testament sources provided for the notion that there will be a "cleansing fire" are 1 Corinthians 3:15 and 1 Peter 1:7, neither of which allude to anything beyond our present world. In both instances, the "fire" being discussed is a metaphorical expression of the trials we may face on earth. This has nothing to do with being refined post-mortem. See the "Catechism of the Catholic Church." Online version, 269.

ultimate decisions about our salvation, or that we could do the same after death, we open the door to all varieties of spiritual perversion and apathy. If we attempt to suggest that salvation cannot actually be altered in this way, then it must be upheld that at least some sort of divine favor could be obtained by invoking the prayers of fallen saints. If true, the desire to spend even more time focusing on the dead abounds, and the system is perpetuated. But we must put Purgatory to the side for just a moment in order to acknowledge that it is not the only view that can lead to this problem. As previously mentioned, many Protestants believe similar things in light of their own spectral fascinations. Though we can all understand the grieving widow who talks to her deceased husband's headstone, experimenting with séances, Ouija boards, and ghost investigations are different issues altogether.

What if the entire system is flawed though? What if my perspective (and others I have mentioned) is correct about the state of the dead? The final result is that "venerating the saints" could be *very* costly. Imagine the poor soul who finds himself stranded on a desert isle, and begins to suffer the effects that tremendous heat exposure and dehydration inevitably lead to. He begins to hallucinate, seeing a lush patch of the greenest vegetation and, buried within it, a pool of crystal-clear water. But as he gets closer and closer to his query, the grim reality of the situation begins to sink in: there is neither a single leafy branch to be found nor a drop of liquid in sight. There is only hot, dry sand, and the certainty that he is now even further away from where he started.

This is a familiar scenario to all of us. Countless songs, books, and movies have popularized this story over the course of time. Though it is often characterized as fantasy, it has happened to far too many weary travelers in reality. I cannot help but wonder: are the theological implications of chasing spirits so very different from the physical results of the man who pursued the mirage? At best, the man ventures farther and farther from safety, making his path out of the desert much more burdensome. At worst, he has travelled too far away to ever make it back home.

PARTING THOUGHTS

First and foremost, I would like to thank those of you who have labored through this book and are finally reading the conclusions. Hopefully, you have found something within these pages that has stirred both the heart and the imagination. While I do not claim to be correct about every single topic that I have evaluated (though I have tried to be), I hope you can appreciate the importance of thinking through the issues of death and the afterlife. As this book draws to a close, I would like to reveal something that may be a bit surprising: as the old saying goes, I don't have a horse in this race. That is, I wasn't overly concerned with whether or not we exist consciously during the interim period when I began my investigation years ago. While I always suspected that the typical way of viewing the issue had holes, I would have been satisfied with whatever conclusion ended up matching the evidence. But be sure: I came to my conclusion—that between the time of death and the resurrection, the dead are unconscious—based on the evidence at hand.

The "evidence" I speak of involves the complete message of the Bible, the thoughts of theologians past, and the overall weight of reason. The truth is that I remain open to the possibility of being convinced otherwise. After all, what difference would it *personally* make if I went to a place of conscious bliss at death or knew nothing of the time between my death and resurrection? In either case, the same amount of time will appear to have passed—none. At the end of the day, one of the major things that separates my view from many others I have discussed is incredibly simplistic. The vast majority of Christians agree that the human soul returns to God when we die. Whether we are talking about heaven, hell, or the places described in Jesus' parable of the Rich Man and Lazarus, the point of contention is mainly about *how* the soul is present with God at this time. In other words, is this a *conscious* or *unconscious* existence?

This basic question is what hundreds of biblical, historical, and logical arguments ultimately lead us towards answering. While that much is simple to understand, the two possibilities have dramatic differences to those of us who are still among the living. Specifically, the attempt to contact the dead—for whatever possible purpose—is apparently no less appealing to Christians than it is to anyone else. Though such a thing is, in my estimation, not possible within any biblical view of the afterlife, the thought remains on the table if the soul consciously survives death. No matter how improbable it may be from a biblical standpoint, the possibility of such interactions has proven to play a major part in the lives of many Christians and their respective church traditions. This is problematic because nothing good can come from a preoccupation with the dead.

Even if ghosts exist, such beliefs lead us to put our trust in things other than the Creator. In this sense, God is robbed of worship. We need only to

148

recall Steven's story in order to see some of the other problems involved in the belief that deceased human beings roam the earth or that they can interact with us in any way. If all the perspectives about the state of the dead were on equal footing—which I certainly do not believe is the case—then I would think that the view which eliminates the prospect of communicating with the dead should be favored above the others. Why support a doctrine that allows these dangers if it is no more plausible than one that does not?

As previously mentioned, I do not believe that Purgatory, the TDP, the identity information view, or any of the like, are all equally tenable Christian perspectives. The entire purpose of this book is to show that the informational view of the soul makes the best sense of things from top to bottom. That said, I am also neither so naïve nor arrogant to assert that a case cannot be made for other perspectives. Many brilliant thinkers, some of whom I have discussed at points within this book, do not agree with my perspective. Many throughout history would not have, either. This does not upset me in the slightest. On the contrary, I openly welcome further discussion on the issue. *I pray for further discussion on this issue.* If nothing else, perhaps this book can begin the process of getting the discussion about the state of the dead and the ultimate hope of the afterlife back on the theological table. It has been far too long that most of us simply accept what we are told concerning these matters. It has been far too long that those who dissent from—nay, those who even dare to question— "tradition" are labeled as heretics or ignorant people.

The truth is that the Bible can potentially lend itself, in some way or another, to any of the doctrines discussed within this book. While that may be true, the goal is to try and discover which view makes the best sense of all the available information. Sure, it would be easy enough to stop after evaluating a couple of verses or a single passage of Scripture. Many do so, of course. Some may take Paul's statement in Philippians 1:23—"I desire to depart and be with Christ, which is better by far"—and interpret it in such a way that it is undeniable; surely, we consciously live in heaven immediately after we die. Case closed, right? On the other hand, others may take something like Hebrews 9:28— ". . . and he will appear a second time, not to bear sin, but to bring salvation to those who are waiting for him"— to its most literal conclusion, and believe that we unconsciously await the resurrection after we die. Again, that settles it.

Similar "cherry-picking" can be done with just about any debatable issue within the Bible. A surface-level reading of Mark 16:17-18 might encourage some to believe that drinking arsenic martinis or playing tag with a black mamba are acceptable ways to prove their faith. Unfortunately, others have attempted even stranger things in the past (think Origen's nether regions).[181] But these are not appropriate interpretations because they ignore the often metaphoric nature of Scripture and the overall weight of the biblical evidence. Again, the critical point is in discerning which view makes the *best sense* of *all* the available evidence; it's about reconciling the whole of the story, while minimizing the mental gymnastics and ungrounded speculations.

If we look at it this way, we may realize that certain passages, such as Paul's statement in Philippians 1:23, lend themselves to other options: options that are actually consistent with views that previously appeared to be contradictory (like mine). Many of the ideas involved in my view are not entirely new or unique—particularly because they began with the biblical authors—and it certainly won't close the book on the discussion of what happens when we depart from this world. The informational view of the soul is my attempt to make the best sense of all the factors—from top to bottom, and everything in between—that we must consider in our search for the truth. Like all other attempts to do so, my view is unquestionably imperfect. I do believe, however, that it makes better sense than the alternatives.

Among the many arguments I have advanced within this book, there are a few that are especially worth remembering. The first is that the entire concept of what makes us living beings excludes the notion that our immaterial component (the soul) can consciously survive by itself; we are not *beings within bodies*. If we are, during the interim period or any other time, then the ancient pagans, Gnostics, Neo-Platonists, and all the like, were correct in their assessment of the issue. By default, the biblical authors and most of the world's best theologians were/are not correct. Remember, those who support the *temporary-disembodiment position* (the TDP) actually do so as a rare (and to me, contradictory) exception to the rules of the body-soul relationship. Hopefully, I have demonstrated this point throughout the book.

The second major item to remember is that our ultimate destinies are supposed to be decided at the general resurrection and the judgment. The Bible nowhere speaks of multiple judgments (in the ultimate sense), and the

---

[181] The early church father Origen is believed (by some) to have castrated himself. It is speculated that he did so on the basis of a very literal reading of Matthew 5:29-30. Refer to "Origen of Alexandria: Life, Works, Thought and Resources" for more about Origen.

entire premise of a great judgment is negated if that were actually the case. The last point is about the nature of the physical body. If we are able to live in heaven or Abraham's bosom as disembodied spirits, then the addition of a tangible body becomes almost superfluous. While most biblical scholars go out of their way to prove that the physical body is essential for life in this age and the next, they often make an obscure exception for the time between the two. In simplest terms, body-soul unity is completely unnecessary if the soul exists as *its own* separate being. The unity is either essential, or it is not. It either takes a body and a soul (identity information) to make us who we are, or it doesn't.

Though I have advanced many arguments throughout the book, these three form the foundation of my position. These arguments are based on the overall weight of Scripture and reason, and though some of them have been made (to some extent) throughout history, none of them have been explained away. With this being said, it should have become apparent within these pages that the issue of what happens when we die is not black and white. In truth, it is just about as complex as anything we could ever imagine. At the very least, I hope that those who care about the truth of this matter will see that my view—and others that affirm an unconscious interim period—is not of Satan; there are a vast number of reasons to accept it as a legitimate explanation of the various issues that exist within the state of the dead discussion.

While the view of unconscious existence in death has certainly never disappeared, mainline Protestants and Catholics alike still largely appear to be appalled by the idea. As mentioned earlier, the reasons for this opposition are somewhat understandable. For most people, it is tremendously comforting to believe that their loved ones are now watching over them from heaven. To some degree, I can definitely resonate with that idea. Like anyone else, I have lost loved ones over the years. But theological discussions should not be about affirming what we are most comfortable with. Theologian William Crockett put it well when he said, "Emotional arguments can be persuasive . . . but we do not derive our doctrine from them."[182] There are plenty of hard truths within the Christian faith that are, nevertheless, still *truths*. I believe that everyone should weigh, measure, and evaluate all of the materials available to them and come to their own conclusions on the matter. We cannot simply

---

[182] William V. Crockett, *Four Views on Hell*, 174.

trust that our pastors, teachers, friends, or relatives have it right based on their education or their spiritual merits. Even the sincerest believer can be wrong.

If we learn anything at all from the Bible, it is that the majority view (which is the TDP, in this case) is not always the right one. We need only look at Jesus' many interactions with the religious elite of his day to understand this point. Further, we must realize that the issues discussed within this book are both complex and mysterious; they warrant an honest, personal investigation. I would again add the caveat that raw emotions should not be the overriding factor in this search for the truth. Regardless of whatever view on the state of the dead one chooses to adhere to, we would do well to remember that no *conscious* time will elapse between our lives here on earth and our future glory with Christ. In this, the fear that our deceased loved ones may not presently exist in heaven should be relinquished, as we are truly free to let the evidence be our guide. In the end, all of us who share a common faith in Jesus Christ can affirm the words of the apostle Paul in solidarity—to live is Christ, and to die is gain.

BIBLIOGRAPHY

Achtemeier, Paul J., Green, Joel B., Thompson, Marianne Meye. *Introducing the New Testament: Its Literature and Theology*. Grand Rapids, MI: William B. Eerdmans Publishing Company, 2001.

Aquinas, Thomas. *Summa Theologica*. Christian Classics Ethereal Library. http://www.ccel.org/ccel/aquinas/summa.pdf

Andrews, Glenn. "What Is Conditional Immortality? - Afterlife." Afterlife. N.p., n.d. Web. 15 Dec. 2014. http://www.afterlife.co.nz/2008/featured-article/what-is-conditional-immortality/

Ball, Bryan W. *The Soul Sleepers: Christian Mortalism from Wycliffe to Priestley*. London, England: James Clarke & Co, 2008.

Bacher,Willhelm, Hirsch, Emil G., Lauterbach, Jacob Z. *JewishEncyclopedia:"Samuel." http://jewishencyclopedia.com/articles/13079-samuel*

Barclay, William. *The Parables of Jesus*. Louisville, KY: Westminster John Knox, 1999.

Beasley-Murray, George R. *New International Bible Commentary: Based on the NIV*. Ed. F. F. Bruce. Grand Rapids, MI: Zondervan, 1979.

Beasley-Murray, George R. *New Bible Commentary*. 21st Century Ed. Downers Grove, IL: InterVarsity Press, 1994.

Behe, Michael J. *Darwin's Black Box: The Biochemical Challenge to Evolution*. New York, NY: Free Press, 1996, 2006.

Biema, David Van. "Christians Wrong About Heaven, Says Bishop." *Time*. Time Inc., 07 Feb. 2008. Web. 23 Apr. 2015.

Bemporad, Jack. "Soul: Jewish Concept." *Encyclopedia.com*. HighBeam Research, n.d. Web. 12 Dec. 2014. http://www.encyclopedia.com/article-1G2-3424502917/soul-jewish-concept.html

Borchert, G.L. "Gnosticism." *Evangelical Dictionary of Biblical Theology*. Ed. Walter A. Elwell. Grand Rapids, MI: Baker, 1996. N. pag. Print.

Burge, G.M.. "Day of Christ, God, the Lord." *Evangelical Dictionary of Biblical Theology*. Ed. Walter A. Elwell. Grand Rapids, MI: Baker, 1996. N. pag.

Burns, Norman T (1972), *Christian Mortalism from Tyndale to Milton*. Cambridge, MA: Harvard University Press, 1972.

John Calvin Tracts & Letters-Psychopannychia." Godrules.net, n.d. Web. 15 Dec. 2014.

"Catechism of the Catholic Church." *United States Conference of Catholic Bishops*. N.p., n.d. Web. 17 Nov. 2014.

Ciampa, Roy E., Rosner, Brian S. "The Structure and Argument of 1 Corinthians: A Biblical/Jewish Approach." *New Testament Studies*. 55.2 (2006): 205-218.

Clement. *The First Epistle of Clement to the Corinthians*. Translated by J.B. Lightfoot.

http://www.ewtn.com/library/patristc/anf1-1.htm

Clouse, R.G. "Millenium, Views of the." *Evangelical Dictionary of Biblical Theology*. Ed. Walter A. Elwell. Grand Rapids, MI: Baker, 1996. Print.

Constant, Eric A. "A Reinterpretation of the Fifth Lateran Council Decree *Apostolici regiminis* (1513)." https://www.msu.edu/~constan8/FifthLat.pdf

Conti, 'Religio Medici's Profession of Faith', in Barbour & Preston (eds.), *Sir Thomas Browne: the world proposed*, p. 157 (2008).

Craig, William L. "What Happens When We Die?" *ReasonableFaith.org*. Web. 06 Nov. 2014. http://www.reasonablefaith.org/transcript/what-happens-when-we-die

Craig, William L. "Is the Cause of the Universe an Uncaused, Personal Creator of the Universe, who sans the Universe Is Beginningless, Changeless, Immaterial, Timeless, Spaceless, and Enormously Powerful"? *ReasonableFaith.org*. Web. 10 Oct. 2010. http://www.reasonablefaith.org/is-the-cause-of-the-universe-an-uncaused-personal-creator-of-the-universe

Crenshaw, James L. *Old Testament Wisdom: An Introduction*. Atlanta, GA: John Knox Press, 1973.

Crockett, William V., Hayes, Zachary J., Pinnock, Clark H., Walvoord, John F. *Four Views on Hell*. Grand Rapids, MI: Zondervan, 1996.

Cullmann, Oscar. "Immortality of the Soul or Resurrection of the Dead?" *Religion Online*. N.p., n.d. Web. 12 Dec. 2014.

Dillard, Raymond B., and Tremper Longman. *An Introduction to the Old Testament*. Grand Rapids, MI: Zondervan, 1994.

D'Souza, Dinesh. *Life After Death: The Evidence*. Washington D.C.: Regnery Publishing, Inc. 2009.

Ehrman, Bart D. *God's Problem: How the Bible Fails to Answer Our Most Important Question--why We Suffer.* New York: HarperOne, 2008. Print.

Elwell, Walter A. *Evangelical Dictionary of Biblical Theology.* Grand Rapids, MI: Baker, 1996.

Fee, Gordon P. *The New Interpretive Commentary on the New Testament: The First Epistle to the Corinthians.* Grand Rapids, MI. William B. Eerdmans Publishers, 1987.

"Fifth Lateran Council 1512-17 A.D." http://www.papalencyclicals.net/, n.d. Web. 19 Dec. 2014.

Fowler, James A. "FLESH: What Does the Bible Mean by the Term "flesh"? *Christ in You Ministries*, 1999. Web. 17 Dec. 2014. http://www.christinyou. net/pages/flesh.html

Fowler, Tara. "Little Boy Who 'Came Back from Heaven' Says He Made It Up." *PEOPLE.com.* N.p., 16 Jan. 2015. Web. 21 Jan. 2015. http://people. com/books/alex-malarkey-little-boy-who-came-back-from-heaven-reveals-hoax/

Fragments of Papias from the Exposition of the Oracles of the Lord. Roberts-Donaldson Translation. http://www.earlychristianwritings.com/text/papias.html

Goodrick, Edward W., John R. Kohlenberger, and James A. Swanson. *Zondervan NIV Exhaustive Concordance.* Grand Rapids, MI: Zondervan Pub. House, 1999.

Grudem, Wayne A. *The First Epistle of Peter: An Introduction and Commentary.* Leicester, England: Inter-Varsity, 1988.

Habermas, Gary R., and James Porter Moreland. *Beyond Death: Exploring the Evidence for Immortality.* Wheaton, IL: Crossway, 1998.

Hilbert, Martin. "How much information is there in the world?" *ScienceDaily.* 11 Feb. 2011. https://www.sciencedaily.com/ releases/2011/02/110210141219.htm

"Immortality of the Soul in the Bible? A Brief History of Conditional Immortality and Answers to Critics." *Afterlife.co.nz* http://www.afterlife. co.nz/2010/theology/articles-c-i/immortality-of-the-soul-in-the-bible/

Immortality of the Soul -. JewishEncyclopedia.com, n.d. Web. 13 Nov. 2014.

"JewishEncyclopedia.com." *SAMUEL.* JewishEncyclopedia.com, n.d. Web. 21 May 2015.

Kamimura, Naoki. *"Augustine's Understanding of the Soul, the Immortality, and the Being in De Immortalitate Animae."* Academia.edu, 5 June 2013. Web. 16 Dec. 2014.

Kantzer, K.S. "Paradise." Evangelical Dictionary of Biblical Theology. Ed. Walter A. Elwell. Grand Rapids, MI: Baker, 1996.

Kent, H.A., Jr. "Paradise." *Evangelical Dictionary of Biblical Theology*. Ed. Walter A. Elwell. Grand Rapids, MI: Baker, 1996.

Keener, Craig S. *The IVP Bible Background Commentary: New Testament*. Downers Grove, IL: InterVarsity, 1993.

Kotsko, Adam. "The Resurrection of the Dead: A Religionless Interpretation." *The Princeton Theological Review XVII*, No. 1.44 (2011): 37-48. Web. 10 Dec. 2014. http://www.princetontheologicalreview.org/issues_pdf/current.pdf

Koukl, Greg. "The Intolerance of Tolerance". Presentation at the 10th Annual EPS Apologetics Conference, Berkeley, CA, (November 17-19, 2011).

Lightner, R.P. *Evangelical Dictionary of Biblical Theology*. Ed. Walter A. Elwell. 2nd ed. Grand Rapids, MI: Baker, 1996.

Lorenzi, Lorenzo. *Devils in Art: Florence from the Middle Ages to the Renaissance*. Florence: Centro Di, 1997.

D. Martin Luthers Werke, Weimar 1883-1929.

http://www.lutherdansk.dk/WA/D.%20Martin%20Luthers%20Werke,%20 Weimarer%20Ausgabe%20-%20WA.htm

"Luther's 95 Theses (A.D. 1517). Carm.org. https://carm.org/luthers-95-theses.

Martin Luther, "An Exposition of Salomon's Booke, called Ecclesiastes or the Preacher (translation 1573)". Reformed Thinkers.

http://reformed-thinker.blogspot.com/2011/02/martin-luther-defense-of-soul-sleep.html

Martyr, Justin. *Fragments of the Lost Work of Justin Martyr*. Robert-Donaldson EnglishTranslation. http://www.earlychristianwritings.com/text/justinmartyr-resurrection.html

McGrath, Alister E. *The Christian Theology Reader*. Oxford, UK: Blackwell, 1995.

Meyer, Stephen C. "Not by chance: From bacterial propulsion systems to human DNA, evidence of intelligent design is everywhere." *Discovery Institute*. Dec. 10, 2005. https://www.discovery.org/a/3059

Moore, David W. *Three in Four Americans Believe in Paranormal*. Gallup, 16 June 2005. Web. 20 May 2015.

Moreland, James Porter, and Scott B. Rae. *Body & Soul: Human Nature & the Crisis in Ethics*. Downers Grove, IL: InterVarsity, 2000.

Morris, Leon. *The First Epistle of Paul to the Corinthians: An Introduction and Commentary*. 2nd ed. Grand Rapids, MI: Wm. B. Eerdmans, 1985.

Morris, Leon. *The Tyndale New Testament Commentaries: Luke.* Grand Rapids, MI: William B. Eerdman, 2002.

Mounce, William D. *Mounce's Complete Expository Dictionary of Old & New Testament Words.* Grand Rapids, MI: Zondervan, 2006.

"New Testament Greek Lexicon." *BibleStudyTools.com.* N.p., n.d. Web. 09 Dec. 2014.

"New Research Explores Teenage Views and Behavior Regarding the Supernatural." Barna Group, 23 Jan. 2006. Web. 20 May 2015. https://www.barna.org/barna-update/5-barna-update/164-new-research-explores-teenage-views-and-behavior-regarding-the-supernatural#.VVyqTVI8rkc.

Origen of Alexandria (c.185 - C.254). *Origen of Alexandria: Life, Works, Thought and Resources.* Religion Facts, n.d. Web. 18 Dec. 2014.

"Origen, Unorthodox Church Father." www.ovrlnd.com/index.php, n.d. Web. 16 Dec. 2014.

Philpott, Kent. "The Third Heaven: The Apostle Paul and Kat Kerr." Earthen Vessel Journal, Sept. 2013. Web. 07 Jan. 2015.

Plaisance, Christopher A. "The Transvaluation of the 'Soul' and the 'Spirit': Platonism and Paulism in H.P. Blavatsky's Isis Unveiled". *The Pomegranate.* 15.1-2 (2013) 250-272 http://www.academia.edu/5071297/The_Transvaluation_of_Soul_and_Spirit_Platonism_and_Paulism_in_H.P._Blavatskys_Isis_Unveiled

Porter, Laurence E. *New International Bible Commentary: Based on the NIV.* Ed. F. F. Bruce. Grand Rapids, MI: Zondervan, 1979.

Prestidge, Warren. *"Asleep in Christ | The Death State - Afterlife." Afterlife.* N.p., 12 Apr. 2013. Web. 15 Dec. 2014. http://www.afterlife.co.nz/2013/publications-conditional-immortality/asleep-in-christ-the-death-state/

Schmithals, Walter, and John E. Steely. *Gnosticism in Corinth: An Investigation of the Letters to the Corinthians.* 2nd ed. Nashville: Abingdon Press, 1971.

Schultz, Carl. "Spirit." BibleStudyTools.com. Baker's Evangelical Dictionary, n.d. Web. 16 Dec. 2014.

"Strong's Greek: 4983. σῶμα (sóma) -- 142 Occurrences." *Strong's Greek: 4983. σῶμα (sóma) -- 142 Occurrences.* Bible Hub, n.d. Web. 21 May 2015.

Tarnas, Richard. *The Passion of the Western Mind: Understanding the Ideas that Have Shaped Our World.* New York, NY: Ballantine Books, 1993.

Tertullian, *adversus Marcionem* III.xxiv.3-6. *Oxford Early Christian Texts: Adversus Marcionem.* Ed. E. Evans. Oxford: Clarendon Press, 1972.

Tertullian, *On the Resurrection of the Flesh*. Early Christian Writings. http://www.earlychristianwritings.com/text/tertullian16.html

Turner, James T Jr. "We Look for the Resurrection of the Dead: An Analytical Theological Rethinking of the Intermediate State and Eschatological Bodily Resurrection in Christian Theology." The University of Edinburgh, 2015.

https://www.era.lib.ed.ac.uk/bitstream/handle/1842/11742/Turner2015. pdf?sequence=2&isAllowed=y

Wesley, John. "The Sermons of John Wesley - Sermon 112," Wesley Center Online.

http://wesley.nnu.edu/john-wesley/the-sermons-of-john-wesley-1872-edition/sermon-112-the-rich-man-and-lazarus/

William Tyndale, *An Answer to Sir Thomas More's dialogue*. Parker's 1850 reprint. https://books.google.com/books?id= E M c O A A A A I A A J & p g = P A 2 & d q = # v = s n i p p e t & q = Purgatory&f=false

Witherington III, Ben. *Revelation and the End Times: Unraveling God's Message of Hope*. Nashville TN: Abingdon Press, 2010.

"Where is the World's Data Being Stored?" *Mozy*. https://mozy.com/infographics/where-is-the-worlds-data-stored/

Wright, N. T. *Surprised by Hope: Rethinking Heaven, the Resurrection, and the Mission of the Church*. New York: HarperOne, 2008.

Uram, Mike. "Jewish Ghost Stories and the Walking Dead." *Philly.com*. N.p., 23 Sept. 2014. Web. 18 Dec. 2014. http://www.philly.com/philly/columnists/mike_uram/Rabbi_Uram_Jewish_ghost_stories.html

Printed in the United States
By Bookmasters